BETWEEN ETERNITIES

Between Eternities

And Other Writings

Javier Marías

Translated from the Spanish by
Margaret Jull Costa

Edited with an Introduction by
Alexis Grohmann

VINTAGE INTERNATIONAL
Vintage Books
A Division of Penguin Random House LLC
New York

A VINTAGE INTERNATIONAL ORIGINAL, AUGUST 2018

Compilation copyright © 2017 by Javier Marías
English translation copyright © 2017 by Margaret Jull Costa
Introduction copyright © 2017 by Alexis Grohmann

Library of Congress Cataloging-in-Publication Data
Names: Marias, Javier, author. | Costa, Margaret Jull, translator. |
Grohmann, Alexis, editor, writer of introduction.
Title: Between eternities / Javier Marias ; translated from the Spanish by
Margaret Jull Costa ; edited with an introduction by Alexis Grohmann.
Description: New York, NY : Vintage, 2018. | A Vintage Books original edition—
Verso title page. |
Identifiers: LCCN 2017060284 (print) | LCCN 2018005901 (ebook) |
ISBN 9781101972106 (ebook) | ISBN 9781101972113 (paperback)
Subjects: LCSH: Marias, Javier—Translations into English. |
BISAC: LITERARY COLLECTIONS / Essays. | LITERARY CRITICISM /
European / Spanish & Portuguese.
Classification: LCC PQ6663.A7218 (ebook) | LCC PQ6663.A7218 A2 2018 (print) |
DDC 864/.64—dc23
LC record available at https://lccn.loc.gov/2017060284

Vintage International Trade Paperback ISBN: 978-1-101-97211-3
eBook ISBN: 978-1-101-97210-6

Author photograph © Riccardo Musacchio and Flavio Ianniello

www.vintagebooks.com

Printed in the United States of America
10 9 8 7 6 5 4 3 2 1

Contents

Contents

DUSTY SPECTACLE

Contents

THOSE WHO ARE STILL HERE

Introduction

"Go on, Go on Thinking"

A Family

Javier Marías's parents, Dolores (Lolita) Franco and Julián Marías, were fervent readers, scholars and writers. They met at university in the 1930s, during the turbulent years of Spain's Second Republic, and Lolita gradually set aside much of her scholarly work to bring up her sons, although she continued to be intellectually active and later published a significant book on Spain seen through its literature. Javier was the fourth of five sons (the firstborn, Julianín, died tragically at the age of three and a half in 1949 and has been movingly evoked by Javier Marías in *Dark Back of Time* and by Julián Marías in his memoirs). Julián Marías was a philosopher, teacher, writer and intellectual. A disciple and friend of Spain's greatest philosopher, José Ortega y Gasset, he was a truly upright and principled person, gentle in private, religious, but at the same time politically progressive. He had the misfortune of looking for the political middle in a period of extremes and blind party loyalty, and his profound dedication to his country rendered him incapable of going into exile, as so many of his contemporaries did after the outbreak of the Spanish Civil War in 1936 and the establishment of Franco's dictatorial regime from 1939. Julián was equally incapable of complicity with the dictatorship. Though he had forged affiliations with the Second Spanish Republic, he was denounced on mostly false charges at the outset of the Franco regime by a treacherous friend, was subsequently imprisoned and only escaped the firing squad thanks to an honest witness called by the prosecution (Javier has described this incident in the first novel of his trilogy, *Your Face Tomorrow*). He suffered reprisals thereafter, was shunned by the establishment and by Spanish universities and travelled to the United States to undertake teaching at various universities there, occasionally accompanied by his family. Thus, Javier spent the first year of his life in Massachusetts, at Wellesley College (as he recalls in "Air-Ships"), where he was to return many decades later to teach a course on Cervantes's *Don Quixote*, and another period in New Haven, when his father worked at Yale. During Spain's transition from dictatorship to democracy in the 1970s and '80s, as Senator by Royal Decree and in discussions with the then young King Juan Carlos I and President Adolfo Suárez in particular, Julián Marías contributed to the careful reform and democratization of Spanish society, as well as to the drafting of the Constitution of 1978.

His sons Miguel, Fernando, Javier and Álvaro grew up in a house brimming with culture, books and paintings—from an early age, Javier had to learn to wrestle with his parents' books in order to make space on the floor to play with his toy soldiers (see "The Invading Library")—as well as a constant stream of visitors, ranging from North American exchange students (his father also taught U.S. students on their year abroad) to writers, artists and intellectuals. Javier and his brothers thus received a lively and extraordinarily open-minded, progressive and international education, both at home and at the uniquely secular, liberal and coeducational Colegio Estudio, in stark contrast with the dominant nationalist, Catholic, regressive and repressive tendencies of the dictatorial regime and all its institutions. Their upbringing was therefore in many ways quite uncommon and privileged, but this privilege had been gained by Lolita Franco and Julián Marías at a high personal, professional and financial cost—although they never spoke of it like that—through their unwavering uprightness and independence of mind and character.

"Don't specialize," they counselled their sons, "learn about everything." And while it may not be surprising, given their family background, that all four sons have made a name for themselves in the sphere of the arts and humanities—as film critics, art historians, musicians and music critics or writers—it is perhaps Javier Marías who has heeded this advice most.

A Novelist

Beyond Spain, Javier Marías is best known as one of Europe's foremost writers, author of fifteen novels translated into forty-four languages and published in fifty-seven countries, with over a dozen, mostly international, literary prizes to his name and eight and a half million volumes of his work sold worldwide. As someone who started writing at the still tender age of fourteen in 1965—his first short story, "Life and Death of Marcelino Iturriaga," was published in a Barcelona newspaper three years later—and who, at the age of fifteen, wrote his first novel (*The Day Before*, unpublished), he quickly emerged as a budding author, publishing *The Dominions of the Wolf* and *Voyage along the Horizon* at the ages of nineteen and twenty-one, respectively, while he was still studying English literature at university in Madrid and translating and coauthoring film scripts for both his uncle and his cousin, the filmmakers Jesús Franco (evoked in this collection) and Ricardo Franco, as well as occasionally working as a production assistant and extra in some of their films (once as a Chinese man).

The Dominions of the Wolf bears witness to this fascination with cinema, and these two early novels were his way of rejecting the realist mode of writing that had characterized much of Spanish literature up to that point and trying to break with the Spanish literary tradition more generally, by renouncing Spain as a theme and any form of Spanishness in narratives set exclusively outside of Spain and populated solely by non-Spanish characters, North American and European, in turn. Both are deliberately imitative, of foreign cinema (Hollywood comedies, melodramas, gangster movies and films noirs of the 1930s, '40s and '50s) and Edwardian literature (Henry James, Joseph Conrad, Arthur Conan Doyle), respectively, and are also one of the main reasons why, for many decades, Javier could not shake off the epithet of "goddamn Anglosaxonist" (as he reminds us in "Chamberí").

The other reason is that after publishing these two novels, in a conscious decision to further his literary apprenticeship, he dedicated the following few years almost exclusively to translating English-language literature (prose and poetry) into Spanish, specifically, works by John Ashbery, W. H. Auden, Sir Thomas Browne, Joseph Conrad, Isak Dinesen, William Faulkner, Thomas Hardy, Edith Holden, Vladimir Nabokov, Frank O'Hara, J. D. Salinger, Wallace Stevens, Robert Louis Stevenson and W. B. Yeats. His most notable translation is undoubtedly that of Laurence Sterne's *The Life and Opinions of Tristram Shandy, Gentleman* (his favourite work of literature, as he explains in "My Favourite Book"), which earned him Spain's National Translation Prize in 1979. It had a great bearing on the development of his writing, not least its digressiveness (a subject he tackles in "Roving with a Compass"). Three more novels followed, in which Marías continued to hone his prose, before he left Spain in 1983, taking up a fixed-term appointment as lecturer at the University of Oxford, where he taught in the Sub-Faculty of Spanish, a sojourn that inspired his 1989 novel, *All Souls* (see "Who Is Who?"), the work that established him as one of Spain's most noteworthy writers, and the novelistic leap that landed him squarely within the world's republic of letters. From then on, his stature has continued to grow with *A Heart So White* (1992), *Tomorrow in the Battle Think on Me* (1994), *Dark Back of Time* (1998), *Your Face Tomorrow* (*1: Fever and Spear*, 2002; *2: Dance and Dream*, 2004; *3: Poison, Shadow and Farewell*, 2007), *The Infatuations* (2011) and *Thus Bad Begins* (2014).

An Essayist

Within Spain, however, Javier Marías is nowadays no less renowned for his essays, including articles and feature writing and, particularly, his weekly newspaper columns, which he has been publishing every Sunday since 4 December 1994 (except for the Sundays of the month of August when he takes a holiday). It is to this Javier Marías that the present collection seeks to introduce the reader. Drawing mainly on the pieces Margaret Jull Costa has translated over the years for the *New York Times* and the *Threepenny Review*, we have included a series of texts of a personal or autobiographical nature (they make up the first part, *A Borrowed Dream*), instances of travel writing or "anatomies" of the character of cities he has lived in (*The Most Conceited of Cities*), pieces of a wide-ranging miscellaneous nature (*All Too Few*), a section on books and literary matters (from second-hand books and bookshops, to why he shies away from computers and still does all his writing on a typewriter: *Dusty Spectacle*) and one on cinema (*Those Who Are Still Here*).

While not attempting to be wholly representative—his collaborations in the press and periodicals date back to the 1970s and amount, in total, to well over a thousand pieces, and we have, for example, omitted many more specialized texts on football, language or overtly political matters—this selection does allow us to discover someone whose all-encompassing gaze seems to have been directed at everything under the sun. So, in one part alone (*All Too Few*), he tackles topics as varied as those of neighbours and their mysterious noises; the plight of a dead stork; the perils of book signings ("Lady with Bombs"); Berlusconi ("No Narrative Shame"); football ("The Weekly Return to Childhood"); a generalized obsession with recovering the bones of the dead ("All in Our Imagination"); and even imagines liberal gun laws in the EU ("A Horrific Nightmare"). In "In Praise of the Egotist" he argues that egotists are among the few capable of seeing the truth; elsewhere, he explains "Why Almost No One Can Be Trusted"; and he sympathetically and sensitively talks about the grief "that dare not speak its name" experienced by mothers when "a long period of their existence is coming to a close, and their life will never be the same" ("All Too Few"). Marías writes here with a voice, a world-view and a prose style quite different to those of his novels and more akin to those of the "father" of the genre Marías cultivates, the sixteenth-century essayist Michel de Montaigne.

Marías's essays are the product of someone who thinks and judges for himself, unconstrained by preconceived ideas, and whose starting point is, in Montaigne's well-known formulation, "What do I know?," rather than "What am I supposed to know?" He says what he thinks about the topics he touches on without censoring himself for fear of causing offence or reprisals of any kind. (There have been a few. To name but one, the first of his subsequently many pieces on the Catholic Church, all very critical of the institution, was suppressed in 2002 by the supplement that housed his columns at the time, *El Semanal*. He objected to this act of censorship, seeing it as too reminiscent of Francoism, and did not hesitate to terminate his collaboration with that publication.)

Not unlike Montaigne, Marías gives us the fruits of his readings, his experience of the world and his reflections on it, and treats, as has been said of Montaigne, "the deepest subjects in the least pompous of manners." His essays share Montaigne's search for truth, keenness of observation, humour, intimacy, informality and human morality, as well as a great range of interests. It has been said that Montaigne, despite his profound engagement with philosophy, Latin and Greek texts, was a gentleman, not a scholar; Marías, too, writes his pieces as a gentleman, a citizen, rather than as a novelist or academic (let's not forget that he taught literature and translation at Oxford, Wellesley and at the Complutense University in Spain, and that in 2007 he was elected a member of the Real Academia Española, Spain's Royal Academy). Marías's voice emerges, as did that of his sixteenth-century predecessor, as a sane voice in a world that, in his view, has gone mad.

It is in this vein, then, that he "talks" to us on paper. Thus he often recalls the past and the dead, paying homage to family, friends and admired artists or writers, such as "the blackest sheep of his family"—there were, apparently, a few—his Uncle Jesús, the above-mentioned film director Jesús Franco, who had a considerable influence on the cinematic and sentimental education of the young Marías; the second King of Redonda, John Gawsworth (whose kingdom Marías would end up inheriting), and his desolate final days ("Too Much Snow"); the ghosts of Joseph Conrad and Juan Benet; Vincent Price, "The Supernatural Master of the World," who "succeeded in doing what few actors in any genre have managed to do, namely, he gave us the immediate, unequivo-cal impression that he had a past, that he was once quite different from the person he appears to be"; George Sanders, "The Man Who Appeared to Want Nothing"; or Ann-Margret, with whom he had his "first platonic" or, in fact, "frustrated carnal love affair," "frus-trated" only "because of the very different dimensions in which we moved, her and me" ("Earthly Sighs"). In the opening piece of our collection, Marías recounts a dream of his brother's that prompts him to speculate that his deceased parents and Julianín are now reunited not only in a tomb, but also in a territory, the past, "which doesn't seem so very dreadful: it's a time, or possibly a place, full of inter-esting people, as well as some who are much loved," he concludes.

In "The Lederhosen," prompted by some old photographs (including one in which he is wearing said shorts or short trousers), he revisits the past and discovers that "the adult we are was already contained in the child that we were." This insight has guided Javier Marías in his relations with others to such an extent that: "Often, in order to get a sense of someone with whom, sooner or later, I'm going to have dealings, I try to imagine what they would have been like as a child and how we would have got on, whether we would have been good friends or have hated each other's guts."

In the same, personal, opening section, he reveals his humorous disregard for the profession to which he belongs: he tells us that hav-ing to wrestle with hefty tomes by philosophers and writers in order to make room for a game of bottle-top football or toy soldiers accus-tomed him from an early age "to negotiating the words of the great philosophers and writers" and led him to lose all respect for anyone who writes, himself included: "Having too much respect for the kind of individuals who partially soured my childhood and invaded the territory occupied by my thrilling games of bottle-top football would seem to me masochistic in the extreme," he says. That may also be why he has never thought of himself as a professional writer.

His love of toy soldiers, incidentally, has not diminished: they are still aligned along most of his bookshelves in his home and study. The reason they do so, he explains in "This Childish Task," is that he does not want to lose sight of the fact that those childhood games are probably one of the origins of his chosen career. Comic books are another origin, which for him and many boys of his generation were companions and teachers, instead of being frowned on as a lesser art; "They weren't called 'graphic novels' then, a term invented by those who feel ashamed of writing or drawing them and, therefore, ashamed of having been a source of pleasure and fantasy for many children and grown-ups, as well as being partly responsible for the literary vocation of many writers, including myself" ("A Hero from 1957"). Javier Marías does not hesitate to criticize such pretentiousness, prejudice or, indeed, the megalomania of artists, writers and critics (real or resulting from their representation—see "Damned Artists!"). In his wonderful essay on film music, "Music for the Eyes," he berates critics and academics for their (our) prejudices, which lead to blindness in judgements:

> Artistic prejudices are always the most difficult to root out. Critics— whose duty should be to see beyond the pretensions of artists and the public's passing fancies—often allow themselves to be persuaded by the way authors present their work, by what they say they have achieved, or else are guided by whatever has been a wild success— usually in order to take the opposing view—and which has been damningly labelled "popular." So, in literature, it has taken almost a hundred years since the death of Robert Louis Stevenson for critics and scholars to consider his work to be "serious" and to notice that

one of his greatest admirers was Henry James, a writer who has always been venerated in academic circles. The fact that Stevenson wrote several brilliant novels enthusiastically devoured by children and adolescents—especially *Treasure Island*—was enough for him to be despised and for those same critics to forget that he was also the author of *Dr. Jekyll and Mr. Hyde* and other extraordinary tales, as well as essays that were far more penetrating and profound than any written by the very critics and professors who dictate what does or does not deserve to be studied and respected.

He has often defended many instances of what in critical or academic circles used to be—or still is—frequently dismissed as popular or mass culture not on a par with other artistic endeavours. So, he has repeatedly championed not only film music or comics, but also allegedly lesser literary genres such as comic novels (by his contemporary Eduardo Mendoza, for example), adventure stories (by Stevenson, Dumas or the best-selling Arturo Pérez-Reverte), ghost stories, stories of the supernatural, or children's literature, going against conventional wisdom more often than not.

He has done this in his essays, but also as a translator—in the 1980s he cotranslated and edited a collection of ghost stories by little-known figures in English literature (*Cuentos únicos /Unique Short Stories*)—and as a publisher, for after becoming King of Redonda in 1997, Xavier I founded his own publishing house (as king he recovered his original name, pronounced in the same way as "Javier"), Reino de Redonda, for which select small imprint he chose to have translated volumes of lesser-known supernatural narratives by Richmal Crompton, *The House* and *Mist and Other Stories*, and by the duo Erckmann-Chatrian (*Les Contes du bord du Rhin*). (He has occasionally paid homage to Crompton, whose William

Brown had such an influence on so many writers of his generation in Spain.) Let us also not forget, in this context, that the literary character he would most like to have been is Sherlock Holmes. His magnificent defence of the cinematic genre of the Western, laid bare in a number of articles in the final section of this volume, is another example of this tendency, as is his formidable championing of *It's a Wonderful Life* and *The Ghost and Mrs. Muir* as ambitious, ambiguous, intense and complex masterpieces of cinema.

Indeed, it is in his essays on cinema that Javier Marías is often at his lucid, corrective and combative best. Here he will attack, for example, as he does often in his writings, the new puritanism, political correctness or pusillanimity that has taken hold of our societies, as he does when he speculates on the demise of the Western in "The Hero's Dreadful Fate":

> Perhaps it's because the Western, as a genre, has traditionally embodied attitudes and behaviour—which it always took seriously, without ever falling into caricature—that now seem shocking to the hypocritical mass of entrenched goody-goodies, who desperately want to dissociate themselves from a whole range of passions that have been common to humanity throughout the ages. For example, in the Western, nobody looks askance at hatred, ambition, the desire for revenge, the determined pursuit of an enemy, the wish to hurt or kill that enemy, the search for redress and sometimes justice for a wrong committed.
>
> [. . .]
>
> Our society does not accept that all men and all women are different. It does not accept that while some are horrified by what they are obliged or choose to do, others are not, and are prepared to bear whatever responsibility or sentence falls to them. It believes, rather,

that everyone should think the same or at least abstain from doing what the majority deem reprehensible. It does not accept that some crimes are not as criminal as others, depending on who commits them and against whom, depending, too, on why. Society knows all about hatred, envy and revenge, but prefers to clothe itself in virtue and pretend ignorance . . .

Javier Marías's lucidity is such that he is able to see and discover things that are there, so to speak, but which many of us have failed to notice or, indeed, things that we do, in fact, recognize, but have never put into words, certainly not so clearly and eloquently. And that is because he keeps looking at the things of this world long after most of us have turned away, and never contents himself with what he has already seen or thought. In *Your Face Tomorrow: Dance and Dream*, Javier recalls his father, Julián Marías, saying, "Go on, go on thinking," and urging his children "to keep on looking at things and at people, beyond what seemed necessary." And that is what we see Javier Marías doing, lucidly, funnily, movingly, brilliantly in *Between Eternities*.

Alexis Grohmann, 2017

A BORROWED DREAM

A Borrowed Dream

Although I'm no great fan of people telling you their dreams, especially when characters in a novel or a film do so—why are they telling me this, I wonder, if it's only a dream and we're in the middle of a fiction anyway—today, I'm going to tell you about a dream told to me by my oldest brother, Miguel.

He had the dream five days after the death of our father, who took his leave of this world on 15 December 2006 at around ten o'clock in the morning. When Miguel described the dream to me, I sensed in his account some of his professional and private obsessions, because, although he's an economist, he's best known as a film critic, and I was aware in his description of various "influences": Lubitsch (*Heaven Can Wait*), Powell and Pressburger (*A Matter of Life and Death*), Mankiewicz (*The Ghost and Mrs. Muir*, one of my all-time favourites) and even Capra (*It's a Wonderful Life*). Anyway, in the dream, Miguel saw our mother, who died in the early hours of 24 December 1977, sitting on a bench in La Dehesa, which is the name of the pretty park in Soria, a city where we spent many a childhood summer. My father came strolling along one of the avenues and stopped in front of her; sitting on her knee was our brother, Julianín, the oldest of the five brothers, who died on 25 June 1949 at the age of three and a half, except that in the dream he didn't actually appear to Miguel (who was the only one of us to have known him) in physical or corporeal form;

3

he was simply there unseen. And then my mother addressed these playful words of reproach to my father: "Honestly, Julián," she said, "fancy taking nearly twenty-nine years to get here. Do you have any idea what it's been like, alone all this time with a three-year-old? Come on, you hold the little inquisitor for a while and be in charge of answering his questions. You know what children his age are like, they never stop asking questions, why this and why that. He's quite worn me out." My father picked up the ethereal child in that awkward way so familiar to us, the four surviving brothers, Miguel, Fernando, Álvaro and myself, rather as if someone had placed in his hands a pile of plates and he could find nowhere to put them down. Anyway, he tried to justify his delay by saying: "I meant to come much sooner, almost straight away, but you know how it is, Lolita, one thing leads to another, and there were books to write, and people kept pestering me to do this and do that. So up until now, I simply haven't had a chance." As with Julianín, my parents were both the age they had been when they died, so my mother, who, in life, had been a year older than my father, appeared in the dream with her sixty-three years and my father with his ninety-one years. "It's odd, isn't it," said our mother, "now I'm much younger than you are. And don't worry, I know what you're like, always in such a hurry when it comes to your own affairs, but with all the time in the world when it's someone else."

It was several nights since he'd had the dream, and Miguel could really only remember snippets, but apparently my father reported to my mother what had happened in her absence and, she, quite contradictorily, on the one hand, listened to him with great interest, and on the other, kept telling him that she knew all about it already ("Don't go thinking I don't know what's been going on"). "There's only one thing I would reproach you with," she said, smiling, "the fact that none of the boys is religious." I don't know about my brothers' beliefs, because we never talk about such personal matters, but it might be true, because I understand there were some mutterings among certain pious, gossipy friends of my father when, at the two masses held after his death, none of us went up to take communion. And my parents, of course, were believers. "Maybe," he said, "but they've all turned out pretty well." "And you could have done more to persuade Javier to get married," was my mother's second, mocking reproach. "Well, he's always been a bit of a butterfly in that respect, as you know, and although it's not quite the same thing, he does seem to have paired up with someone now, a very pleasant, cheerful woman, whom I met in fact." "Several of the grandchildren are paired up too," said my mother, determined to needle him a little more, "but not one of them is married." To which our father responded incongruously and untruthfully: "Well, the thing is, you see, only homosexuals get married nowadays," to which our mother, very well informed on her park bench, retorted: "Don't tell such fibs. Homosexuals can and do get married, it's true, but so can anyone else who cares to."

As often happens in dreams, the scene was a mixture of verisimilitude—of domesticity almost—and the absurd. It amused me to find my father slightly caught on the hop, although for no real reason, poor man, and that he should agree with her that he had delayed far too long in coming to join her. I'm not, in fact, religious, but I do love films, and I particularly like the films I mentioned earlier and other similar ones that feature ghosts or people who continue to feel engaged with what's going on in the world they've left behind, and so I found my brother's dream at once amusing and consoling. There is, after all, a territory—if I can call it that—in which all three, my father, my mother and Julianín, are gathered together, and not just in the same tomb: all three are now the past, a memory, and that, at least, they share in common. And when you think about it, being the past doesn't seem so very dreadful: it's a time, or possibly a place, full of interesting people, as well as some who are much loved.

(2006)

Air-Ships

A few years ago, I wrote an article in which I confessed, in rather jocular fashion, to a fear of flying, even though—with no little show of courage—I board a plane about twenty times a year. I'm pleased to say that I now feel much more confident during flights, perhaps because I've grown used to it or perhaps, as the trail of years behind us grows, we become more scornful about our possible future life and more satisfied with the life we've already accumulated. However, over a period of at least twenty years, plane journeys—of fifty minutes, two, seven or even twelve hours—could be relied upon to transform me into a highly superstitious little boy, who reached his various destinations feeling utterly drained after the hours of tension and the indescribable effort of having to "carry" the plane.

What I've always found so odd about my fears—or is this, perhaps, the explanation—is the fact that I first flew in a plane when I was only one month old, in the days when, for most people, flying was still a rare experience. I was born in Madrid on 20 September 1951, and on that very date—it had been planned beforehand, so it wasn't that he took one look at me and fled—my father set off on the first of his Atlantic crossings and travelled to America with a contract to teach at Wellesley College, Massachusetts—a college for young ladies—for the academic year of 1951–52. My mother followed a month later, taking with her my two older brothers, Miguel

7

and Fernando, as well as me, the newborn baby. I don't know what the travelling conditions were like (apart from the fact that I was all dressed in pink, because they had been expecting a girl), or whether I cried a little or a lot as we crossed the ocean, or whether the crew members of Iberia or TWA made a fuss of me or loathed me. And I recall nothing either of the return journey—New York–Madrid—nine or ten months later. I do, however, have a vague recollection of my third trip by plane. I was just four years old, had acquired another brother, Álvaro, and my father had decided to take us all to New Haven, Connecticut, at the behest of Yale University. It's not a very pleasant memory: I can see myself—not crying, but very, very angry—lying in the aisle, refusing to get up and doubtless obstructing crew and passengers alike. I don't know how long the tantrum lasted—possibly a couple of minutes, possibly much longer—but I'm sure that if, as an adult, I had seen the child that was me, I would have hated him for blocking the aisle; more than that, I would have thought it a bad omen, which is always rather worrying when in mid-flight.

It's probably a well-known fact—although I can't be sure because people don't talk about it much—that those of us who suffer in planes tend to invest a great deal of feverish, exhausting mental activity in our role as, how can I put it, "imaginary copilots." As I said, my fear of flying is now abating, but throughout my life I've spent many hours on board in a state of permanent alertness, attentive not only to any possible changes of mood in the engines, or to the plane's recognizable or unexpected noises, or to its scheduled or unscheduled ups and downs, but also to everything else around me, in particular the air hostesses and the stewards and even the captain's variable tones of voice over the intercom—whether he sounds calm or nervous. I have tended to see "signs" or "premonitions" in the tiniest details and, given that all superstitions are arbitrary, it always used to make me feel uneasy if a passenger stood talking in the aisle for too long, especially if he or she was Japanese, don't ask me why. Nor was I soothed, particularly on long-haul flights, by the sight of other excessively relaxed and uninhibited passengers, who, far from keeping a close eye on our flight path, as is the duty of all caring and committed travellers, laughed and drank, moved around the cabin, played cards or performed other equally grave and reckless acts, or so it seemed to me. In short, I spend or spent the entire journey "controlling" and "helping" and "protecting" the whole hazardous crossing with my tireless thoughts. A four-year-old child blocking the aisle would definitely have strained my nerves. I'm not sure I would have been able to refrain from giving him a good slap. No, I would doubtless have contained my irritation because since I reached the age of shaving, I've always behaved myself onboard planes, unlike the callow creature I was then. I have limited myself to keeping a firm grip on an open newspaper (of the broadsheet variety, so that there's no chance of my sneaking a glance out of the windows), either pretending to read it or actually reading it—although without taking in a single word—meanwhile fending off any attempts at conversation (one doesn't want to become distracted and neglect one's duty as lookout), demolishing at high speed whatever food is placed in front of me, and all the while clutching some wooden object I've brought with me for the purpose, since there doesn't tend to be any wood—a major oversight—on those flying submarines.

It was a similar remark, made in that earlier article, and my subsequent confession that I'd worn out the wooden toothpicks and matches I grasped between my fingers, that provoked a charming Iberia air hostess into sending me a letter and a little wooden key ring in the form of a plane, so that, in future, I wouldn't have to make a fool of myself abroad, holding those grubby matches and toothpicks. And that same air hostess, as well as recounting a few anecdotes from her long experience in the air, made me think of planes, for the first time, as relatively "humanizable" objects, which one could, in a way, and depending on the circumstances, mentally direct. Not that there's anything very remarkable about that. Indeed, it's perfectly normal. She told me in her letter that, whenever the plane she was on lurched or bumped about a bit or jolted, she would issue a silent order: "Down, boy!" Yes, an order, an exorcism, a persuasive word.

In *The Mirror of the Sea*—a magnificent book that I translated into Spanish several years ago now—the great Polish-English novelist Joseph Conrad speaks of ships having their own character and spirit, their own norms of behaviour, their caprices, rebellions and gratitudes. Of how, in large measure, their performance and reliability depend on the treatment they receive from captain and crew. If treated with respect, affection, consideration, care and tact, a ship, says Conrad, is grateful and responds by trying hard and giving of its best (or, rather, *her* best, since curiously and significantly the only objects that merit a gender in the English language are ships, which are always referred to as "she" and not, as would be more natural, as "it"). If, on the contrary, the relationship between them is one of superiority, disdain or is simply too demanding, authoritarian or neglectful, abusive, inconsiderate or even despotic, ships react badly, and feel no "loyalty" and fail to "protect" their crews at moments of risk or danger. "Ships," writes Conrad, "are not exactly what men make them. They have their own nature; they can of themselves minister to our self-esteem by the demand their qualities make upon our skill and their shortcomings upon our hardiness and endurance." And further on, he adds: "The love that is given to ships is profoundly different from the love men feel for every other work of their hands—the love they bear to their houses, for instance—because it is untainted by the pride of possession. The pride of skill, the pride of responsibility, the pride of endurance there may be, but otherwise it is a disinterested sentiment. No seaman ever cherished a ship, even if she belonged to him, merely because of the profit she put in his pocket. No one, I think, ever did; for a ship-owner, even of the best, has always been outside the pale of that sentiment embracing in a feeling of intimate, equal fellowship the ship and the man, backing each other against the implacable, if sometimes dissembled, hostility of their world of waters." And later still, Conrad describes the touching words, tantamount to a funeral oration, uttered by the captain of a brig that had sunk: "No ship could have done so well . . . She was small, but she was good. I had no anxiety. She was strong. Last voyage I had my wife and two children in her. No other ship could have stood so long the weather she had to live through for days and days before we got dismasted a fortnight ago. She was fairly worn out, and that's all. You may believe me. She lasted under us for days and days, but she could not last forever. It was long enough. I am glad it is over. No better ship was ever left to sink at sea on such a day as this." Conrad sums up by saying: "She had lived, he had loved her; she had suffered and he was glad she was at rest."

We air passengers are not accustomed to perceiving, or even imagining, planes in this way, as almost animate beings, with a capacity for suffering and endurance, requiring consideration and esteem, and being sensitive, almost, to gratitude and rancour. We board them and can barely distinguish between them, we know nothing of their age or their past history, we don't even notice their names, which, in Spain at least, are chosen in such a bureaucratic, pious spirit, so lacking in poetry, adventure and imagination, that it's hard to retain them and, therefore, recognize them if ever we entrust ourselves to them again. I would like to ask Iberia, in this, the twenty-first century, to abandon their anodyne patriotic gestures and adulatory nods to the Catholic Church—all those planes called *Our Lady of the Pillar* and *Our Lady of Good Remedy*, *The City of Burgos* and *The City of Tarragona*—and instead choose names that are more cheerful and more literary. I, for one, would feel safer and more reassured, more protected, if I knew I was flying in *The Red Eagle* or *The Fire Arrow* or even *Achilles* or *Emma Bovary* or *Falstaff* or *Liberty Valance* or *Nostromo*.

Perhaps reading that air hostess's epistolary revelations had something to do with the diminution of my fears. Until that comment of hers, it had never occurred to me that captains might have a similar relationship with their planes as old seadogs do with their ships, and that air crews are like sailors. Perhaps what surprised and disturbed me during my long watches as a fearful traveller—a murmur, a squeak, a bump, a lurch—are perfectly recognizable to them, familiar, customary, the reactions of each individualized and distinguishable plane, just as we recognize the people close to us by their gestures and intonations, their silences and vacillations, so much so that, often, we don't even need them to speak to know what's wrong, what's going through their minds, what they're suffering or worrying about or plotting or waiting for.

This possibility soothes me. We live in an age that tends to depersonalize even people, and which is, in principle, averse to anthropomorphism. Indeed, such a tendency is often criticized, erroneously and foolishly in my view, since that "rapprochement" between the human and the nonhuman is quite natural and spontaneous, and far from being an attempt to deprive animals, plants and objects of their respective selves, it places them in the category of the "humanizable," which is, for us, the highest and most respectable of categories. I know people who talk to, question, spoil, threaten or even quarrel with their computers, saying things like: "Right, now, you behave yourself" or thanking them for their help. There's nothing wrong in that, it's perfectly understandable. In fact, given how often we travel in planes, the odd thing about our relationship with them—those complex machines endowed with movement, to which we surrender ourselves, and that transport us through the air—is that it *isn't* more "personal" or more "animal" or more "sailor-like," if you prefer. Perhaps those who crew them haven't known how to communicate this to us. I've never seen them pat a plane, as you might pat a horse to calm or reward it; I've never seen planes being groomed and cleaned and tidied, except very hurriedly and impatiently; I've never seen them loved as Conrad's captain loved his sunken brig; I've never seen air hostesses—who spend a lot of time onboard—treat them with the respect and care, at once fatherly and comradely, enjoyed by ships. That's what I would like to see, less cool efficiency and more affection, and I'm sure that I, along with many other tense, vigilant passengers, would become infected by their confidence and be able to relax, because then, planes, like ships in the old days, would have their "reputation," and we would know something of their voyages, their history, their deeds, their past and their future. The pilots, instead of frightening us with their usual litany of cold, hair-raising facts ("We will be flying at an absurdly high altitude, the temperature outside is unbelievably cold," etc.), could say: "This plane, the *Pierre Menard*, has had an amazing life so far. It was born ten years ago, has made five hundred flights and crossed the Atlantic on sixty-three previous occasions. It has always responded well to us, even in the most unfavourable of circumstances. It's a docile plane by nature, but very sensitive as well, why, I remember once . . ." Well, I leave the rest up to the airlines. Perhaps it isn't too much to ask for a little more literature or—which comes to the same thing—a little uniqueness; a little history and background, a little life.

(2004)

The Lederhosen

For reasons I needn't go into here, I recently had to search out some old photographs, in particular photos from my childhood and early youth. I showed some of these to my brothers and to their sons and daughters, my nieces and nephews, most of whom are now in their twenties. And whereas the images of their parents and uncles, as babies or as children, produced in them a mixture of euphoria, retrospective tenderness and hilarity, they provoked, I think, in the subjects of those photographs a rather different combination of feelings: there was occasional hilarity, true, but tinged always, and perhaps inevitably, with a little pity, an occasional dash of embarrassment— a photo taken at an awkward age, or a photo in which one is wearing some particularly dated and thus antiquated item of clothing—and, now and then, a strange sense of simultaneity, or, rather, of immediate recognition and of time annulled. This last feeling occurred mainly when I could instantly recall the exact moment and place when a photo was taken, could remember precisely the circumstances and even my general state of mind, or, more concretely, could "smell" and "feel" the clothes I was wearing. To give one non-incriminating example: when I saw myself in the stout lederhosen of which my godmother Olga brought us all a pair from Germany and which saw us through a whole school year, my immediate thought was: "There I am in *my* lederhosen, with the mother-of-pearl reindeer on the front," and not, as occurred to me with other photos: "There I am in *those* lederhosen . . ." The difference is worth noting: in the first instance, I felt briefly as if I still owned those lederhosen and—even more striking and, of course, more comical—that I could once again put them on as I so often did when I was about eight years old; in the second instance, the aforementioned lederhosen were firmly in the past and I felt no connection with them whatsoever, clear in the knowledge that they were no longer to be found in my wardrobe and that I would never put them on again (not even for some eccentric trip to Bavaria, where even the grown-ups wear them).

I said earlier that when I look at these old photos I often feel a touch of pity. Don't misunderstand me: that word doesn't mean the same as self-pity, which would, in my view, be entirely misplaced. It isn't a matter of thinking how very innocent I was then (although I was, and it doesn't matter what date you put on that "then"); it isn't that I see myself in the light of today and am moved to pity, if I can put it like that, simply because the child or boy I was knows nothing of the troubles that await him, when the truth is he knows nothing of the satisfactions either, and rare is the life that does not contain both things: disappointments and contentments, enthusiasms and regrets. One should avoid harbouring such paternalistic feelings for oneself, largely because they're incongruous and absurd, but also because they're harmful and pointless, not only because it's ridiculous to feel moved by the person one was and, up to a point, still is, but because it implies that one is putting the past in a higher category than the present, and placing ignorance above knowledge. Looking back nostalgically on the days when "you still didn't know" or when "you still believed" or "still hoped" or "still dreamed" only makes sense in an age like ours that glorifies childhood and tries to make it last longer than ever before, even passing on the infection to those who should have long ago left childhood behind. All of us (apart from those who were wretchedly unhappy as children) occasionally have a sense of childhood as our real home, a sense that everything that has happened since was mere accident, sham and artifice, and that the true and original "I" has been succeeded by a series of false "I"s with whom we have very little in common. This has led many a sentimental writer to declare—along with all the other nonsense that gets spouted in interviews—that they "have a child inside them," that "childhood is their one true homeland" and that they live, therefore, in a state of permanent exile.

Any feeling of pity arises, at least in my case, from the contrary idea: far from carrying a child around inside us (which would, it must be said, be a terrible nuisance), what we think we see in our photos or in our oldest memories is that the adult we are was already contained in the child that we were, and wasn't very difficult to spot either. Often, in order to get a sense of someone with whom, sooner or later, I'm going to have dealings, I try to imagine what they would have been like as a child and how we would have got on, whether we would have been good friends or have hated each other's guts. One comes to realize that if anyone contains anyone, it's the child who contains the future adult and not the other way round; and when one looks at old photos, it's hard not to think, in a way, of the burden this implies. Not that there's any place for self-pity here either: throughout all of history children have always been adults in the making, and the reason childhood has been seen as important is because of the way it shapes and influences what will come later, which is what matters. Nowadays, on the other hand, people give importance to childhood itself, as if humanity's sole crazy aim was to shape and create eternal, perennial children. Not a good idea. But that is how it is.

(2005)

An Unknowable Mystery

A few weeks ago, a Sunday supplement published an interview with yours truly, illustrated by three studio photographs taken for the occasion. On the afternoon when I arrived for the photographic session, I wasn't, as I recall, in a particularly bad mood and nothing very dreadful had happened to me. True, I was in a hurry, but I submitted patiently enough to the tedious business of posing and sitting around. The result, from my point of view, was not at all flattering: in all three portraits I look like a horrible, vicious, unpleasant person, not unlike the images they used to print on wanted posters for murderers on the run. A bad-tempered individual whom I myself would hesitate to approach for fear he might turn nasty. A killer. It's true that journalists and photographers take special pleasure in choosing the worst shots and I understand this and know how much it amuses them, just as TV cameras deliberately focus on an interviewee's bald head or on the hole in his sock, or capture the moment when he's scratching his nose or when he sneezes. It is nevertheless true that there was a moment, the moment captured by the camera, when we did look like that, just at one particular moment, in a particular light and from a never-to-be-repeated angle. Those circumstances may well never be repeated and we will therefore never again be that person or appear like that to anyone else, but the same applies to good photos, the ones we feel pleased with and that even flatter us.

The truth is that we don't know what we look like because, among other reasons, we're always changing. Mirrors don't tell us much: we see ourselves the wrong way round, our left eye is our right eye in the mirror and vice versa, and since we're all slightly asymmetrical, our reflected image is very inexact. I always give the example of Cary Grant, who wore his hair parted—very precisely—on the right. If we were to see him as he would have seen himself in mirrors, with the part on the left, he would doubtless seem like a different person entirely. I'm not sure that television or video reproduce us very faithfully either (those of us, that is, who appear on television or own a video camera). The situations in which we're filmed are so artificial that I doubt very much that our ways of speaking or moving correspond to any other moment of our lives—which is to say, most moments—spent without an audience. I hate seeing myself on a screen, I look like such a fraud, which is perhaps why I want to think that it's a false image. And that's despite my trying, on television or in photographs, not to do anything I wouldn't do normally. A little while ago, I refused to be immortalized by a magazine in the act of jumping, arguing that jumping wasn't part of my normal, everyday life. Then they asked me to stand holding a globe of the world in my arms. Again I replied that this wasn't something I would normally do. Finally—they were, of course, looking for an "unconventional" shot—they asked me to take a step forward, and I agreed to that, since I take steps all the time. During a television interview once, years ago now, I was urged to do all manner of silly things: as a young man, I used to play guitar very badly, and so they handed me one to play, but I wouldn't strum a single chord, saying that I might mess it up and how would they explain that to the person who had lent it to them; then, because as a young man I used to perform acrobatics, they asked me to do a pirouette for them right there and then, and again I refused, arguing that if I fell awkwardly, I might wreck the set or break a spotlight. When I shared an apartment with my father, photographers were always fascinated by his study, which was a chaos of papers and books that filled sofas, armchairs and the floor. They always said: "Oh, let's do the photos here, it's got real atmosphere." In vain did I tell them that it wasn't *my* atmosphere and that I was, in fact, extremely tidy. Consequently, there are dozens of images of me buried in books and mounds of paper that had nothing whatsoever to do with me. My study never looks a mess.

It seems that nowadays we all have a fairly clear idea of our appearance, and yet I still hold that this remains an unknowable mystery to us all. It isn't just a matter of how others see us—and they might view us kindly or otherwise—but the fact that we ourselves are often disconcerted and astonished when we see ourselves: "Is that me?" or "Is that what I look like now?" What we should really ask ourselves is why we continue to believe that we stay the same from childhood into old age. I don't think it's ever due to the enigma of our changeable, multiple appearance, but to a convention and to a faculty. That convention is the name we bear and the faculty is memory.

(1996)

Ghosts and Antiquities

It occurred to me a few days ago that it was time I got myself a new address book; the black cover of my old one is badly worn and its contents a real jumble, so much so that any new names beginning with C can be found under E, because C and D have long since been filled up, as have M and R and a few other letters. Faced by this tedious task, I realized that it wasn't, as I thought, just ten or twelve years since I last transferred everything into a new book, but more like twenty-five or thirty. Or perhaps it was simply that I made the same decision then that I will doubtless make now, namely, not to exclude or score out anyone, not even the dead whose phone numbers and addresses I will never use again. It's possible. It's possible that ten or twelve years ago, it seemed to me—how can I put it—disloyal and unfair to suppress those who had once been part of my life, however tangentially or briefly. I see the phone numbers of people who live abroad (always the most transient), people I met once or perhaps never met at all, the kind of numbers your parents or friends give you when you're younger, just in case anything bad happens to you while you're travelling, some mishap, and you have no one else to turn to. I don't even know who some of the names are on these squared-paper pages. Roberto Oltra, Beatrice Brooks, alongside an address in San Mateo, California, a place I've never visited. Then there's Vibeke Munk. I have a vague idea she was a young Danish woman I spoke to on a train journey, who knows where or when. Nelson Modlin and Freddy Melgar, Maria Panos of Massachusetts, Piers Rodgers of London or Valérie Lejeune, I find it impossible to believe that I did once know who they were or to recall why I noted down their numbers on some now lost night that only returns—and yet doesn't return—enigmatic and nebulous, in these names written down in my own hand (and may they all forgive me if I ought to be able to remember them better than I can).

There are other people I do remember, although they're so distant and so diluted that I find it hard to summon up their faces; they merely appeared in my life and then disappeared, as I did from theirs. I see the name of Ángeles Carrasco, a fellow student at college with red hair and blue eyes, a charming, rather gawky young woman, of whom I learned later on—I've no idea from whom, but the fact is there in my memory—that she died falling from a window in a building in Glasgow; whether she jumped, on the other hand, is a fact my memory is unable to verify. I see the name of Roberto Pujadas, an Argentinian I think, who, even though he didn't know me, was kind enough to wangle me a free pass to the Cinémathèque in Paris when I was seventeen; I never saw him again and I learned some years later that he had died; I will never be able to thank him enough for that immense and entirely disinterested favour. I see the name of Laurie Cunningham, the English winger who played for Real Madrid. I interviewed him in English to help out a then girlfriend who knew nothing about football, and he died years later in a car accident. I see the names of Édouard de Andréis and Gilles Barbedette, my first French publishers, a delightful, intelligent couple who died on consecutive days, each after a long illness but from a quite different disease. I see, too, names that have no such sad memories attached, but whose presence is hard to explain. Like those

of Philip and Jane Rylands in Venice, whom I have some recollection
of having visited there, yet I couldn't swear that I know who they
are. There are the names of women who gave me their number in
some bar or other, I suppose, but whom I didn't dare to ring afterwards, or perhaps did, but without success, despite the promising
phone number. Who are Suzanne Weldon and Caterina Visani, for
example? I can't even put faces to their names, whereas I can to
Muriel Sieber and to Mercedes Viviani, although not much more
than that. And there I am as well, with the addresses I had in countries where I lived a long time ago, and which I would have forgotten
had I not found them here: Via della Lupa 4, in Rome; that must have
been in 1975. Horton House, 666 Washington Street; that was in
Massachusetts in 1984. And 22 Woodstock Road, Oxford; an address
I remember much more clearly. You will, I'm sure, understand why
I decided not to copy everything into my new book, but to keep this
list of semi-ghosts, replete with antiquities, growing more jumbled
and more torn with each day that passes. They erase themselves
whether we like it or not and cancel out all vestiges and echoes of
what was once so present and full of meaning.

(2003)

The Invading Library

Like all the other apartments I've ever lived in, the apartment in which I spent my childhood was full of books. However, the word "full" doesn't really come near the truth, neither do the words "crammed" or "crowded," because not only was every wall covered with shelves, each of which was packed with volumes from every imaginable century, but the books also sometimes served as rugs, tables, sofas, chairs and even, almost, beds. I don't mean that there was no furniture in the apartment and that we sat on piles of books or ate from other still taller piles—with a consequent disquieting sensation of constant instability—but that the rugs, tables, sofas, seats and even beds were often buried beneath vast tomes, for example, the complete and very abundant works of the late-Renaissance philosopher Francisco Suárez. I remember those in particular because, on one occasion, I had to wrestle for hours with the philosophers Suárez and Condillac in order to make a large enough space on the floor to play with my toy soldiers. Bear in mind that my size at the time (I was seven or eight) didn't really equip me for the easy removal of those large seventeenth- or eighteenth-century volumes obstructing my innocent games.

In fact, for myself and my three brothers, the house was one long obstacle race—almost two hundred yards long—the obstacles always taking the form of books. That is why, from an early age, I became used to negotiating the words of the great philosophers and writers, with the inevitable result that I have a deep-rooted lack of respect for anyone who writes, myself included. It still surprises me when I see how other people (especially politicians and commentators) kowtow to writers or else fight to appear in photos accompanied by some scribe or other, or when the state rushes to give succour to ailing, ruined poets, privileging them with a treatment that only heaps humiliation on equally ruined or ailing street cleaners, businessmen, waiters, lawyers and cobblers. My scant respect for the trade to which I belong (from the most ancient of academicians to the most youthful of libelists) derives from a childhood home in which, as I have said, I grew used to mistreating and misusing almost all the seminal texts from the history of culture. Having too much respect for the kind of individuals who partially soured my childhood and invaded the territory occupied by my thrilling games of bottle-top football would seem to me masochistic in the extreme.

But to return to the description of my childhood home, things did not stop there. I mean that my parents, not content with that overweening love of books, felt exactly the same about paintings. It's hard to understand how those two loves could be compatible, especially when you consider that there wasn't a blank or empty wall to be seen in my childhood home. The absurd habit of hanging pictures in the bathroom and even the kitchen had not yet arrived, and given that it was the custom then to have two servants (a cook and a maid, who were always at daggers drawn), there was no way that one could set aside a room for paintings (as dentists and notaries do), a kind of mini-museum: the only room that could have been used for this purpose, and the only one in which there were no books, was occupied by the terrible rows between cook and maid, from which, according to some mysterious preordained law of subjugation, the latter almost always emerged the loser. Although, having said that there were no books, I realize now that the room, in fact, contained the two hundred Simenon books carefully and devotedly collected by my father. They were in French, of course, but I suppose it was a case of what later came to be called subliminal warnings, so that the servants wouldn't overstep the mark in their quarrels or be tempted to steal any nonliterary objects when it came to their inevitable dismissal. Inspector Maigret was watching.

Anyway, my parents' pictorial enthusiasm found a method of placing the paintings they acquired on top of the books, using a crazy mechanism that converted the canvases into small hanging doors. The pictures were hung only by their left side, so that they could be easily "opened" to reveal the volumes they normally covered. An excellent copy of Fra Angelico's *Annunciation* by Daniel Canellada, numerous landscapes by the nineteenth-century artist Ricardo Arredondo, an equally large number by the painter and friend of the family Alfredo Ramón, some miniatures by Vicente López, a few portraits by Vázquez Díaz, a few works by Benjamín Palencia and the occasional Eduardo Vicente, all hung absurdly from the highest shelves, thus eliminating from the rooms still more lateral space. I thus became accustomed to seeing paintings hung not against a smooth, white, plain backdrop, but surrounded by the spines and edges of bound volumes, which may be why I have equally scant respect for painters. Indeed, whenever I see a painting in an exhibition or museum, I have to repress an initial impulse to "open" it and "take out" a book by Kierkegaard or Aristotle, as if the pictures were just strongbox doors behind which were to be found the greatest bibliographic treasures. Only after that first impression, which converts any masterpiece into a small decorated door, only then can I concentrate and see what there is to see.

The truth is that, despite all these inconveniences, I still cannot conceive of any comfortable abode whose walls are not carpeted with the brightly coloured spines and edges of books and built-in paintings, and although the various apartments in which I've lived in various countries have always been very temporary and not, of course, mine, I have never been able to feel even minimally at ease in them until I have acquired a few books and placed them on the shelves, a pale reflection of that childhood bounty. Only then have I begun to think of the place in question (be it England, the United States or Italy) as habitable: an apartment is made up of floors, ceilings and walls, and although I prefer the first two to remain uncluttered or, at most, adorned with a rug or lamp, the walls need to be totally covered so that the books can speak to me through their closed mouths, their motley, multicoloured and very silent spines.

(1990)

Uncle Jesús

The only reason why Uncle Jesús, my mother's brother, could not be termed the black sheep of the family was because there had already been so many, quite how many remains unclear, but far more than is advisable for the happiness and serenity of any family (we even count among our numbers a murderer, possibly a mass murderer). Uncle Jesús, however, was by far the blackest sheep of recent generations, at least until I and my cousins were old enough to commit new outrages and felonies.

My earliest memories of Uncle Jesús go back to the time when I was still a child of tender years and he was living with my grandparents in Calle Cea Bermúdez in Madrid. My parents used to take me and my brothers there for Saturday lunch, where the menu never varied: it was what we used to call "Cuban food" and my grandmother, an excitable, cheerful, ironic woman who was Cuban by birth, presented it to us as the only recipe to be had in the whole of Havana. In fact, we saw very little of Uncle Jesús, because he was not usually up by lunchtime. My grandmother, the most mild-mannered of people, would urge us children not to make too much noise because "poor Jesús is sleeping." I assume that the expression "poor Jesús" was a half-conscious attempt on his mother's part to make us (and herself) believe that Uncle Jesús had been working hard all night. Nothing could have been further from the truth:

through his other six surviving siblings, we knew that our uncle was out partying every night until all hours.

Like many small children, I had a highly developed sense of cleanliness and a natural puritanism, and I remember my horror when I saw from the corridor that his bed was still unmade even at that late hour, when he was taking a leisurely bath while we were having our aperitif. Jesús occasionally joined us for those "Cuban lunches," always whistling or humming, with his wet hair carefully combed, although at other times, he would race straight from the bathroom out into the street, doubtless fleeing the horde of children. When he did stay for lunch, he was always very funny and clever, as was his brother Javier, who was a couple of years younger and the baby of the family. Like my grandfather, several of my uncles could play the piano or some other instrument (Jesús, I seem to recall, could knock out a few jazz classics, jazz being his great love), and they would enliven our lunches there with occasional mad sorties to the piano—which happened to be located in the dining room—on which, between courses, they would hammer wildly away. The macabre tendencies of both Jesús and his older brother Enrique (now a respected music critic) were already apparent even at that early age, for they took delight in frightening their junior siblings—Tina (aka Gloria) or Javier—by singing a little ditty, the words of which also reached our young ears. I can now remember only the gruesome opening lines: "A nice little boy all roasted and toasted/is what I like best for my lunch,/some bones and a lung,/a nose and some tongue/slip down with a slurp and a crunch." While they were singing, they would stare fixedly at us younger children and lick their lips. I see in this a clear musical antecedent to Jesús's later cinematographic liking for vampires and Jack the Rippers.

After a certain age, however, I preferred it when Uncle Jesús wasn't there, leaving the field clear for me. For despite being forbidden from entering his room, or precisely because of that, I would spend all afternoon inspecting it at great length. And my inspections became longer and longer when I discovered the magnificent collection of erotica that Jesús kept hidden away in his wardrobe. You have to remember that I'm speaking here of the early 1960s in Spain, when it was even rarer to see a photo of a woman's breast than to see one in the flesh (either by chance or thanks to some particularly uninhibited or provocative maid). Jesús's collection was a veritable treasure trove for the preadolescent I was then, and the item I enjoyed most was an unusual book (a hardback with full-page spreads) dedicated entirely to photographs of Brigitte Bardot, in which she never appeared wearing more than one article of clothing and usually less. Uncle Jesús may not know it, but I owe him a great debt of gratitude for this early initiation.

To a large extent, I also owe him my initiation into literature, because, at the age of seventeen, I ran away to Paris to write my first novel, *The Dominions of the Wolf*, with the inestimable collaboration of the person who was, by then, more Jess Frank than Jesús. Tardily and after much delay, he had married a beautiful Frenchwoman called Nicole and, at the time, owned an apartment in Rue Freycinet, near the Champs-Elysées, which he was generous enough to let me use as my writing base in the summer of 1969, while he was away filming. It was an excellent place, presided over by a white grand piano and by shelves crammed—no need for concealment now—with pornographic books and magazines. I suppose, by then, Jesús had a good excuse for having such a collection—assuming his French wife needed him to provide her with an excuse—because as well as making horror and adventure films, he also made skin flicks, which were, I believe, filmed mainly in Germany and Italy under extravagant pseudonyms probably unknown to anyone, and he doubtless needed those publications as a source of new talent.

Those were the years when I saw most of him and when he behaved most like the tolerant, errant uncle all the nephews of the world deserve. One summer, he also lent me the apartment he had in Rome, in Viale dei Parioli, where the big-name film directors lived, including Vittorio Gassman and Sergio Leone. He even took me with him filming: in one of his Fu Manchu films, my cousin Ricardo Franco and I appear in a couple of shots, looking totally unrecognizable. Disguised as Chinese hoodlums wearing black silk outfits and red headbands and wielding swords, we raced barefoot down a precipitous slope to the shore of a lake which was, in fact, a reservoir on the outskirts of Madrid. This suicidal descent, repeated several times, is, I think, the most dangerous thing I have ever done, and I nearly split my head open several times, not that Jesús Franco was bothered (even if the extras were his own flesh and blood), just as long as he got his takes. He made so many films and so quickly that he was, I understand, always working against the clock. I've even heard it said that on more than one occasion, without the knowledge of the actors, whom he kept in a state of confusion by giving them strange, bewildering scripts, he shot two films at once, with the same team and cast, who thus, completely unbeknown to them, were doing two jobs, but only getting paid for one. Unfortunately, the film in which I played such an ephemeral role involved none of the great names with whom Jesús was working at the time, for he had joined forces with an eccentric British producer called Harry Alan Towers and had at his beck and call such old glories and legends as Jack Palance, George Sanders, Christopher Lee, Mercedes McCambridge and Herbert Lom, to name but a few. He did, however, regale us with many juicy anecdotes about them.

While Uncle Jesús was a source of joy to us, he was, both before and after that, and over a period of many years, a cause of despair for our parents. When he finally married Nicole, after a long bachelorhood and numerous girlfriends, each more absurd and unspeakable than the last, it was explained to us children that Nicole was a widow, so as to justify the existence of our new cousin, Caroline, who came along with her. Later on, in that summer of *The Dominions of the Wolf*, I happened to meet the father of our false cousin, and he was, I seem to recall, a very jolly divorcé called Jacques. The worst thing, as far as my mother was concerned, were the porn films about which, on the other hand, we heard very little. My mother was the eldest of a family of what started out as eleven children (four died either on the journey or before they had even set off) and she was nearly twenty years older than the three youngest, Tina (aka Gloria), Jesús and Javier, to whom she was a mother long before there was the remotest chance of my brothers and I even being conceived. For that reason, I think, she felt her lecherous brother's cinematographic inclinations to be a personal failure on her part: she didn't so much regret the licentious path his career had taken as see in it a promising moral trajectory cut short. "It doesn't seem possible," she used to say, "when I think how religious Jesús was as a child."

As far as I know, Jesús continued to be pretty much a child, but there was no way my mother could know that. Those who have shared hotel rooms with him recall, as did my mother when she remembered him as a boy, how panicky he would get if no light was left on to protect him from the dark. It's hard to imagine when you see him—a short man, verging on the plump, a nervous, jokey, hyperactive type, with a somewhat flattened nose down which his glasses always seem about to slide. During my adolescence and early youth, no one called me ignorant and uncultivated as often as he did. Whenever he mentioned some C-list actor or some obscure figure from the jazz world, and I asked who they were, he would indignantly get to his feet and shout: "You mean you don't know who Willis Bouchey is? How can you possibly not know Joe Albany?" And so on and so on, as if it were a universal duty to know who those people were: "You really don't know who Jack Pennick is? You're having me on. You don't know who Ike Quebec is?" And he would exclaim in astonishment: "Ike Quebec! Willis Bouchey! Jack Pennick! Joe Albany! What ignorance! And you call yourself cultured! But they're really famous! It's like not knowing who Cervantes is!" I should add that if I ever did find out who the very celebrated Albany, Bouchey, Quebec and Pennick were, I did so by my own means, because beyond feigning amazement, expressing a very real indignation and gesticulating wildly, Uncle Jesús never deigned to tell me.

(1991)

Old Friends

It's odd how, over time, one loses touch with certain friends, especially groups of friends. With individuals it's easier to trace the process that led to that rift, an argument perhaps or an insurmountable difference of opinion; with others it was more a slow drift of disillusion, when the person to whom you felt very close for a time evolved in such a way that he or she became a stranger or, worse, someone you despised or found boring (or else we were the ones who "deteriorated" and were more or less rejected). This must have happened with a lot of people of my generation (politicians and journalists for the most part), who were very idealistic and combative at university, but ended up at the opposite end of the spectrum: "reinterpreting" the Civil War, tacitly rehabilitating Francoism or doing property deals with what they termed "pragmatism," but which was really just cynicism pure and simple. One sometimes learns, with horror and desolation, that a friend of many years—once you stop viewing them as kindly as you used to—now, quite implausibly, represents everything you most hate. Or else you hear him defending the ideas, attitudes and people he loathed fifteen or even ten years ago. I don't mean that people shouldn't change and adapt and modify and come to see things differently, but there are limits that "converts" fail to respect, a long path that needs to be travelled: what I find unacceptable are sudden transformations, as if by magic: now

I'm here and now I'm over there, without anyone seeing how I arrived at that new position.

Far more difficult to understand are the cases where, if I can put it like this, nothing happened: there were no betrayals, no disenchantments or quarrels, not even a sense of weariness. When one of those old friends who you haven't seen for ages dies, time somehow concertinas, and what seemed remote only a few days before the sad news broke suddenly becomes intensely clear. This happened when Michi Panero died, some years ago now, and I just couldn't understand why we hadn't seen each other for such a long time, when, at the age of nineteen or twenty (he was six days older than me, we were born in the same month of the same year), we saw each other every day: after morning classes and after lunch, I would go over to his tiny apartment in Calle de Hermosilla (a great privilege at that age), and we would decide what to do, taking it for granted that whatever we did we would do together. I felt the same when I saw the obituary of Gustavo Pérez de Ayala; it was in his mother's apartment in Calle de Padilla that I undertook one of my first paid commissions, correcting and polishing the translation of a book so bad that it naturally enjoyed enormous success, *Love Story*. I am ashamed to confess that he and I were responsible for the Spanish version of that ridiculous saying, which, for a time, became the motto of all lovers: "Love means never having to say you're sorry." I would head over there every evening, and one of those daily friendships was born, one that lasted quite a long time (although when you're young, everything seems to last a long time). When and why did we stop seeing each other, Michi and I, Gustavo and I? I simply don't know.

Later, when I was in my thirties, for a period of years (well, it seemed like years) I used to go out for supper very late (almost never before midnight) to a restaurant called El Café then and possibly La Mordida now, if it still exists. A few of us would simply drop by without ever arranging to do so or announcing our intention: there were bound to be two or three of us present, if not seven or eight, plus a few less assiduous members, who knew where to find us. Among the regulars were: Antonio Gasset, whom I now only see occasionally on my TV screen; and Tano Díaz Yanes, whom I still have lunch with once a month or so—but just the two of us now, and much earlier in the day; the scriptwriter and novelist Eduardo Calvo, who never failed to turn up, has been in Algeria for several years now, running an Instituto Cervantes no one ever visits; Edmundo Gil, that most inveterate of bachelors, has married and has a child, and has left his job as a notary in order to produce films; Toni Oliver, who was the wealthiest among us (he ran a chain of cinemas, at least I think he did; we didn't ask each other many questions), suffered various setbacks caused by unreliable business partners and now, apparently, writes lyrics for the singer Sabina; the doctor, Charlie, who didn't seem at all like a doctor, is presumably still practising; and as for Julio, the owner of the restaurant, he's still going great guns and has expanded his business. I still often talk to Julia, but I have no idea what happened to Paloma, Isabel, Maru and Natalia. Altogether, I know little about most of them. And yet there was a long period in our lives when we used to have supper together almost every night, and could count on each other's company, and we used to laugh all the time about a hundred thousand things. How is it that none of that exists any more? When did we stop going or who was the first to disappear? That restaurant, if it does still exist, probably still echoes with our endless laughter, like that of the living ghosts we are to each other now.

(2006)

I'm Going to Have Fun

I've written before about Doña Carmen García del Diestro or, rather, Señorita Cuqui, my literature teacher at the Colegio Estudio in Madrid. She is now in her nineties and has asked me to write a few lines for the talk she's going to give at the end-of-term meeting held by the current teaching staff. I decided instead to write a letter and I reproduce it here as a homage not just to her, but to a whole generation of teachers, and because some of what I say could well apply to other professions too.

"This is an age in which teachers, constrained as they are by rules, regulations and other such pedantries, enjoy less and less freedom. This means they are allowed to use their imaginations less and less too, and instead have imitation and uniformity thrust upon them. Some will be glad of this. In every profession there are and always have been lazy, routine-bound people, who like to be told what to do, not just on a daily basis, but throughout their lives, people who want security not adventure, repetition not risk; comforting rules and restrictions that leave no room for the subversive enthusiasm with which they would sometimes have set about their work in the past.

"Perhaps I'm wrong to use the past tense there—I hope so. Their numbers are shrinking, but there still are people who do set about their daily work and even their entire lives with imagination and enthusiasm, preferring not to have everything neatly mapped out before them; people who welcome surprises—even if those surprises are not very pleasant—rather than feeling that their life has been programmed for all eternity. I feel that such enthusiasm—which, inevitably, often flags—and such imagination—you only need a modest pinch of the stuff—are particularly important in education. The times we live in certainly do not help, offering teachers little encouragement or reward, whether political, economic or social. Nevertheless, a teacher's first rule should be: I'M GOING TO HAVE FUN. That was certainly my motto during the few years when, as an accidental impostor, I taught in Oxford, Wellesley and Madrid. And one thing I learned was that if I was having fun, then so were the students. They were intrigued, curious, obliged to think, hoping that, at the end of the class—as at the end of a story—there would be some revelation, some deduction, some not insignificant conclusion, the answer to an enigma or, which comes to the same thing, some fresh snippet of knowledge. It didn't matter if, when the bell went, none of those things had happened, what mattered was their hope and confidence in the process by which some problem or piece of knowledge was transmitted. A fleeting glimpse of a mirage.

"That, I think, is the main thing: teaching others to think, to feel interested and curious, and this can be achieved even in the most arid and least practical of subjects, like mathematics or Latin. But I think, too, that it can only be achieved if the person provoking the thinking, the interest and the curiosity is also enjoying him or herself—even if that enjoyment is short-lived and lasts only as long as the class does.

"You, of course, and many other teachers, especially the teachers at the Colegio Estudio, were the people who convinced me of the truth of what I'm saying now. You were brilliant at all those things, and I'm keenly aware that, for many of you, being a schoolteacher meant abandoning theoretically loftier ambitions, meant resignation and renunciation during a dictatorship that was determined to destroy the hopes and dreams of many Spaniards. I doubt that you had all long nurtured a vocation to be a teacher. Probably many of you hadn't. And some of you would have gone to your classes as if it were a penance. And yet most of you, and especially you, Señorita Cuqui, rose above any setbacks, sorrows or disappointments with your vehement desire to have fun. And you were imaginative and happy, ironic and, for the most part, cheerful, ready to take risks and to be surprised—fortunately for us, especially for me. And I know that if there were no teachers (sitting behind a desk or standing at a blackboard), teachers like the ones I watched and listened to for all those years, the world would be a much sadder, more stupid and less attractive place than the one I was lucky enough to discover. And regardless of how teachers may be viewed nowadays, their main task is still not so much passing on knowledge as shaping their students, which is why their role continues to be such a vital one. And so, for the good of everyone, I trust that there will never be any shortage of teachers who follow both your example and your motto: I'M GOING TO HAVE FUN. Have a very happy and fun meeting."

(1999)

THE MOST CONCEITED
OF CITIES

Chamberí

I was born at No. 16 Calle de Covarrubias in Madrid, which means that despite my reputation as a foreignizer, a traitor to the country and "a goddamn Anglosaxonist" (as one furious now quasi-academic once called me)—a reputation that has dogged me ever since I published my first novel—I come from the most genuinely *madrileño* area of Spain's capital city, namely, Chamberí. I grew up and was educated there and in the surrounding area, and when I moved apartments a few years ago, I didn't stray very far.

There are certain streets in Chamberí that I always associate with my childhood, streets that still exist and have preserved their old names, none of them particularly resonant now, or else the names have simply grown inconsequential because forgotten: Miguel Ángel, Génova, Sagasta, Zurbano, Luchana, Zurbarán, Almagro, Fortuny, Bárbara de Braganza, Santa Engracia. And Covarrubias. The streets may still exist, but, in large measure, they have also been destroyed. That area, which is now home to so many banks, was once full of small eighteenth-century palaces and mansions with high doors and imperial marble staircases. I certainly didn't live in one of those, but they were the backdrop to the walk I went on most frequently with my brothers, hand in hand with my mother and with Leo, our highly imaginative maid, who had us believe that she was the girlfriend of the football player Gento (a popular idol at the time)

43

and told us apocryphal stories about Laurel and Hardy. Or else with two worthy ladies of Cuban origin and accent, my grandmother and her sister, Aunt María, who would accompany us, complaining and excited, to one of the nearby cinemas. Almost none of these remain. They all had monarchical names: the Príncipe Alfonso, the María Cristina, and the Carlos III, which still survives. Another cinema, the Colón, lasted into my adolescence, its name dating from after the Civil War, when it replaced that of the Royalty, which was clearly too "goddamn Anglosaxonist" for Francoism.

Younger taxi-drivers are greatly surprised when I ask them to take the "*bulevar*" route, when there has been nothing in Madrid for decades now that you could even jokingly refer to as a boulevard. But that is how we people born in Chamberí in the 1950s knew the four streets of Génova, Sagasta, Carranza and Alberto Aguilera, which are now an indescribable flood of cars driven by hardened criminals. When I was a child, the street was a polite and respectful place, occupied by spruce, gleaming automobiles, which their owners would drive almost apologetically, and by enormous black taxis with tip-up seats—*traspontines* or *transportines* as we children called them—that we fought over the privilege of sitting in. It was, of course, also a city of trams, trolleybuses (trolleybuses!) and double deckers, exactly like the London ones, except that they were blue and had the entrance on the right, despite having been made in Britain, where the door is on the left. Racing up the spiral stairs to the top floor was like a daily adventure, and helped us to identify more closely with the characters created by Richmal Crompton or Enid Blyton, childhood heroes who never disappointed. Nor was it unusual to see carts drawn by mules or donkeys and piled high with boxes and battered furniture or a rolled-up carpet on end; these were driven by *traperos*—junkmen—who for some reason (whether it was mere chance or out of a desire to be ornamental I'll never know) were always accompanied by some extremely beautiful, pale-eyed, gipsy-ish girl, sitting with her back to the driver and therefore facing the trams or taxis patiently following behind. That's why it still always thrills me to see a female face looking out of the back of some passing vehicle, although nowadays those faces tend to lack all mystery, they're mostly gum-chewing fifteen-year-olds with frozen smiles, who always go around in a gaggle and are never alone, not like the solitary female passengers of those carts.

Madrid, or, if you prefer, Chamberí, was to the eyes of a child a city dominated by cake shops and grocery stores, places of abundance and even good taste. Of the latter, the nearest, which still exists, had one of the loveliest names I have ever seen on a sign: Viena Capellanes. From another, Mantequerías Lyón, a boy came every day to the house to deliver our order, because it was inconceivable then that you would buy food to be eaten on any day other than the one on which it was bought. In the midst of all this industrious refinement, it was not infrequent to catch a very strong whiff of cow as you walked down the street. As a small child, I found it easy enough to crouch down and peer through a barred window to find a few of those illustrious mammals crowded together in a cellar. In order, I suppose, not to besmirch the city's reputation as the capital of Spain, those dairies were called *lecherías* not *vaquerías* (naming the product, "*leche*," rather than the source, "*vaca*"), despite the astonishing and very obvious presence of those beasts just two steps away from the trolleybuses. And so, incredible though it may seem, what with the mules and donkeys of the junkmen, the cows and horses with their riders that could also be seen sometimes trotting along certain streets (Ferraz, Génova, Cea Bermúdez), we children of the 1950s rubbed shoulders on a daily basis with creatures typical of

nineteenth-century cities. My memory of that Madrid is of an unhurried, orderly city (perhaps excessively orderly, for I've never seen
more policemen on the streets anywhere), and perhaps because I was
a child and was more aware of other children, I remember its human
landscape as being dominated by two things: by girls in blue or grey
uniforms or wearing a red jersey and wrinkled socks, with books
and files clasped to their incipient bosoms, as they shuffled along
through the helter-skelter rush of children; and by the elegance that
was expected of any woman living in that typically Madrid *barrio*, so
much so that *piropos* (the comments addressed by men to women in
the street) were almost obligatory, although always decorous. I still
remember something a man said to my mother one Sunday when I
was walking back with her after mass: "You're the loveliest thing
I've ever seen, in miniature." My mother burst out laughing, and
was, I remember, wearing one of those decorative combs Spanish
women often used to wear in their hair.

(1990)

The Most Conceited of Cities

One of the innumerable ways of differentiating large cities would be to divide them into the boastful and the conceited, in the certain knowledge that there isn't a city in the world that doesn't fit one of those two categories. It might seem, at first sight, that the categories are too alike, inhabit the same semantic area, that the frontier between them is too blurred and, therefore, pointless. For me, though, there is a big difference, which has to do, above all, with character, because ultimately, it is character—far more than the look of a place or the customs of its inhabitants—that leaves its mark on you as a visitor and stays with you when you leave.

Boastful cities tend to be insecure, childlike and chatty (even vociferous), unenigmatic and exhausting, impatient places eager for praise and in a hurry to captivate. If you don't watch out, they'll take you on walkabout or plunge you into the hustle and bustle and thus not allow you, as a visitor, to go poking around on your own account and at your own pace; they'll try by every means possible (however disrespectful or loutish) to impose their own wishes on anyone who dares to tread their streets. In other words, they try to draw you in, to subdue and overwhelm you. Boastful cities like Paris or Rome or Madrid are completely changed by the presence of foreigners, not so much because they rely on them (if that were the case, they wouldn't be so boastful), but because they simply cannot leave them in peace to do their own thing. It could be said that the only reason they pay them any attention at all is in order to intoxicate, stun, befuddle and even corrupt them as much as possible. Their boastfulness definitely has a totalitarian streak: they don't allow for difference or even distance, for impartiality or the cool spectator's eye. They are all-pervading and require wholehearted commitment, they demand it, and yet they are the ones doing the committing.

Barcelona, on the other hand, is the most conceited city I know. Even more so than San Sebastián or London, even more than New York or Venice. This category of city shares with the other category a belief in its utter uniqueness—either for some specific reason or as a whole. Nevertheless, the attitude and character of conceited cities isn't just different, it's diametrically opposed. They are far surer of themselves and, therefore, lazier. They are also more enigmatic, more reserved and more elusive. True, they couldn't live without praise, but they prefer envy. They like to hold back, to appear unassailable, knowing that there will always be people wishing to assail them. They never do anything for the visitor, they don't even bother or pester you, and, unlike boastful cities, they put up with you as a thing apart and resist any show of commitment or adherence. They are conscious of bestowing a great honour on visitors and expect this to be duly repaid not just with compliments, but with amazement and unconditional surrender.

What makes Barcelona an even more conceited city than its colleagues is that, surprisingly, and unlike them, it doesn't even go to the trouble of embarking on the elegant and discreet task of attracting visitors—which, however passive, is still a task. San Sebastián seems to be always dressed up to the nines in case some unexpected visitor should call, mindful that there is always a chance it might be seen; London betrays its chronic nervousness and coquetry in its conservatism and the ban it has imposed on changing anything, like those people who refuse to alter their hairstyle because they once made a memorable conquest while sporting the one they have; New York attracts by cultivating an ever closer resemblance to the preconceived image one has of it, gleaned from the movies; Venice not only never changes a single brick, it spends all its time gazing at itself as if there were nothing else to do in the world, thus redoubling the attention lavished upon it anyway; meanwhile, Barcelona appears somehow unaware of its abilities or else is simply much better at pretending, and that is what makes it the most conceited of cities. This greater presumption consists not only in never even thinking of formally soliciting the admiration or respect of others, but—unlike those other cities—in never even appearing to expect it.

That is why Barcelona can, at certain moments and in certain ways, seem a lukewarm or even inhospitable city. I have always seen it, rather, as an excessively modest, overly respectful place, possessed of the kind of conceit you can sense, but which barely reveals itself, or so very bashfully that it appears to be receiving any flattering remarks unwillingly, patiently and with a stiff smile, as if it were a trial that has to be endured in order not to appear impolite. Or perhaps its conceit is a purely internal affair: it is far more interested—possibly uniquely so—in securing the devotion of its own offspring, and whether or not this is accompanied by the devotion of visitors is of secondary importance. What could be more conceited than someone who only truly values his own opinion or has such a lofty idea of himself that his own approval is the only approval he wants?

If one described a person in such terms, they would seem narcissistic or, worse, self-absorbed. And yet the attitude and character of Barcelona is, in my view, neither of those things. It is, I feel, more to do with focus, self-discipline and reserve, like someone immersed in an experiment or some task of great consequence. It is, for example, the only Spanish city (of those I know) that seems to take its own traditions, fiestas and customs perfectly seriously and unironically: on St. George's Day, its inhabitants buy a rose or a book, and on St. John's Night, they eat *coca de San Juan* (a traditional kind of cake containing candied fruit and pine nuts). And they do this simply because they still think it's a good thing to do, regardless of whether anyone else knows that they're doing it, and never in a spirit of parody or exhibitionism or twee folkloricism, as happens almost everywhere else nowadays with celebrations that have their origins in the past.

This idea of doing things even though no one else knows about them provides a useful measure of the city's reserved nature. If one of the ways by which one judges the spirit of a place and its preoccupations is by looking at the kind of shops that proliferate there, Madrid—where I was born and still live—is notable for the crazy abundance of ostentatious banks and filthy drinking dives, alternating with bureaucratic buildings, restaurants, cafés, bars and pseudo-taverns, all of them pretty filthy too. It is notable, in short, for the vulgar display of money and of public and street life, the latter in the form of food and drink. In Barcelona, though, one finds a strange proliferation of shops catering for numismatists and philatelists, along with cake shops and grocery stores, which are known there as *colmados* and in my own city of Madrid by the more anachronistic and visionary term *ultramarinos*. This speaks of a society of consumers and accumulators, but one that does its consuming and accumulating in private: the cakes are usually taken home, as are any purchases made in the *colmados*, and collecting is a very personalized form of accumulating, a very private, individualistic form, not to be confused with anyone else's. One could say that Barcelona is a place in which not everyone aspires to doing and owning the same things, as is generally the case in the rest of Spain, but in doing and owning what really interests them, or more than that, what is unique to them. Not that there is a complete lack of competitive spirit, it simply has its roots in the diverse and the secret, as if Barcelona's inhabitants were aware that the most enviable things are always those whose nature one cannot quite grasp. This is one of the reasons why they are anything but boastful, because telling others what one has achieved or what one owns will only make it easier for those others to do the same, since they will then know what they're looking for, which is always the first step to getting anything. To my mind, the behaviour of its citizens can also be attributed to the city, which does not compare itself with others or worry about what they might or might not do; rather, it follows its own course. There is something almost autistic about this attitude, as if the city knew that curiosity about the outside world can also constitute a threat and a danger: after all, it's very difficult to see without being seen.

The various *barrios* of Barcelona are all quite different, but they mostly share that same suspicious, self-sufficient spirit: the elegant houses in the upper part of the city and the Ramblas, Poble Nou and the Ensanche, San Gervasio and Sarrià, the *barrio gótico* and Gracia. This partly has to do, I think, with something so obvious that no one takes much notice of it: Barcelona is a city on a hill, easy to find one's way around, but in which the view ahead is constantly being interrupted, thus creating the impression of a compartmentalized city, rather than of a continuous, controllable, predictable space; it seems, instead, a perpetual unknown, a permanent secret. I remember the feeling of expectation and unease I always get when I'm walking up some narrow, unfamiliar street, Castañer, for example, which, absurdly, rises perpendicular to the slopes one knows have every right to be steep, those that go from sea to mountain and from mountain to sea. This hill, like many others, is so steep that, even though you know from experience what awaits you at the top, you nevertheless walk up it as if you were climbing some unknown peak or the scaffold. That's how it is in Barcelona, you can't always see where you're going, in fact, you see very little, and when you do get a glimpse of some expanse, some landscape, it's the slope of Tibidabo with its excellent observatory which closes off the horizon as if there were nothing beyond, or at any rate nothing more interesting.

However, it isn't just the famous boundaries imposed by sea and mountain that make the city an enclosed space; Barcelona simply is a very self-contained place that prefers not to display itself. That is why, even for someone like myself, who lived there for three years and is therefore not a mere visitor, it is a somewhat indecipherable city, although without being hostile or inhospitable. This is not (although it certainly helps) because Barcelonians keep both their houses and their collections away from prying eyes and rarely invite people back, nor because half the population have hanging over them the fictitious cloud of those who believe they have for centuries been the victims of injustice and insults, nor that the other half (especially the Andalusians) behave like those fathers or fathers-in-law up from the country who don't know where to put themselves or how to spend their time when they visit their urban sons or daughters-in-law, nor what to make of hobbies or pastimes that seem to hark back to a bygone age: mountain-climbing and hiking, dancing the *sardana* in the middle of the street, or the aforementioned philately and numismatics. In contrast to all this is the frenzied daily life of the streets, which betrays the city's southernness; a possibly feigned innocence, which, nevertheless, dispels the cloud hanging over the half of the population that feels offended and brings a gleam to their eye; a variety of physical types, which is essential to any large modern city if it is to feel breathable; a pleasure in hobbies and pastimes that look to the future: music, books, handsome restaurants and bars, cocktails, graphic art (it's a place where you pause to consider the signs above the shops).

What is indecipherable and enigmatic about Barcelona comes more from that all-pervading introspection: the city looks at itself and neither expects anything nor learns anything apart from what it invents; each shop or business premises aspires to being different, and the best way to achieve this is to ignore all the others; the city's inhabitants establish and jealously guard their respective territories, they avoid mixing or even meeting. I remember saying elsewhere that, however many people you see in the streets of Barcelona (and sometimes you see a lot, although never any *bains de foule*), one always has the sense, tinged with certainty, that inside those inaccessible houses there must be even more people, occupied perhaps in devouring cakes or arranging and studying the stamps and coins in which the city abounds. The most intriguing aspect, though, is that one should feel obliged to imagine such strange, unlikely activities, because, otherwise, there is only a blank or an empty space in one's imagination (what the devil *are* they up to?), populated only by the literary shadows of unscrupulous financiers and scrupulous anarchists intent on their machinations: both of which are ghosts from the past.

For the visitor, Barcelona, especially at night, is like the shop windows at Christmas for Dickensian children. The lights in the houses don't illuminate, even dimly, the passer-by looking in from outside; instead they emphasize the darkness in which he stands pondering the hidden worlds whose unfathomable existence those lights proclaim. As I said before, perhaps that is the greatest possible act of conceit: announcing your presence from afar, but being so confident of your own charms that you feel no need to show yourself.

(1990)

The Keys of Wisdom

To judge by the way my former colleagues at Oxford used to race about during the two years I spent there teaching Spanish literature and translation theory, their university must be the most active in the world and the one with the strictest timetables too. Perhaps it's really a question of geographical distribution, made worse by the size of the city, where almost no distance is great enough to merit taking the car or catching a bus (it seems a waste not to walk everywhere), for in the space of one day, the dons divide their teaching and their knowledge among several colleges and the odd faculty. I think that is why they find themselves obliged to run ceaselessly from one end of the city to the other, which means that when they choose to wear their optional gowns, the city appears to be infested with flocks of low-flying crows, reminiscent of Hitchcock's *The Birds*.

However, most of their work (a great deal of work) is taken up with the so-called tutorials, the one-to-one classes, usually given in the rooms provided by the don's particular college. This would make one think that, contrary to what I have said, these teachers lead a very sedentary life and that it must be the students who spend the day running about, not through the streets, but certainly from one set of rooms to another in the bosom of the college to which they belong. The fact is, though, I never saw a single student running, whereas I was often lashed by the tails of my teaching colleagues' gowns and buffeted by their briefcases as they rushed past. It's fortunate that they rarely ever wear mortarboards now, otherwise the air would be full of flying slates and the dons would need to hold on to their mortarboards with one hand, and having both hands free is of great importance in Oxford, even if only to be able to cope with the many keys required to open the many doors that a don is obliged to go through during the course of the day. I can still recall my surprise and dismay (I could already imagine the holes that the sheer weight of them would make in my pockets) when, shortly after joining the university, I was handed my own bunch of keys, and I never did learn to tell one from the other: two keys for the Spanish library, another for the street door of the building where I had my office, another two for an intervening door, two more for my office door, three or four to get into the Senior Common Room of the Taylor Institution after hours, and another three for my pigeonhole or personal mailbox. In order to accommodate them all, I had to evict some of the usual inhabitants of my pockets, such as lighters and pens, and learn the art of opening highly complex double and triple locks while holding several dictionaries.

Fortunately, I did not have to run as well, since all my activities (lectures, plus some classes hieroglyphically named "Prose and Unseen Classes") took place in the same building, namely the Taylorian or Faculty of Medieval and Modern Languages. I was therefore spared not just the running about, but also the endless work and occasional upsets that tutorials cause the teaching staff. Not only must the dons conscientiously prepare each one-to-one class without the safety net of a full or half-full class in which it doesn't matter if some students are bored as long as there are others who are paying or pretending to pay attention, as happens in the rest

of the university world, they may also suffer the vexation and humiliation of having a student complain about what he considers to be the
deficiencies of the teacher, or even reject out of hand the teacher of
a particular subject because he judges him to be inadequate or to
know not much more than he knows himself. I remember the right-
eous anger of one of my French colleagues when his teaching
services had been declined by a smug American, the son of a diplo-
mat. This colleague is one of the most astute critics I have ever
known, so much so that he has never deigned to publish anything,
not wishing, as he often said, "to contribute more trash with which
to bury literature." This was doubtless a mixture of overstatement
and vanity, since, especially when it comes to producing standard
texts, as well as serious erudition and sensible interpretations, much
of what Oxford publishes in the field of literature is essential to any
student or critic.

Perhaps, though, the real problem is precisely that lack of silliness
combined with a fear of taking intellectual risks. Oxford has a horror
of originality: it gives the impression of suffering from an excess of
common sense, which, if wielded with great acuity, can easily be
used to dismiss any risky theory or interpretation (from Italy or
France, for example), at least in the subjects with which I came into
contact. On more than one occasion, I witnessed the verbal cruci-
fixion, on the part of my colleagues, of some American, Spanish or
even Cambridge-based professor, who had been invited to give a
talk to our seminar. True, these crucifixions were carried out with
enormous delicacy, as if the pain would be lessened if the nails were
hammered in very slowly and by someone wearing silk gloves. The
Oxford dialectical method does not consist, as it does at other universities around the world, in an exchange of more or less contrary
statements, but in a litany of hesitant and extremely polite but

poisonous questions ("I wonder if . . ." is the usual opening gambit) to which no one, however well prepared and composed they might be, will be capable of giving a satisfactory answer. Oxford, then, almost never states, it merely questions, and it does so to perfection.

This attitude is passed on to the students, who, despite the university's increasingly open admissions policy, immediately gain a sense that they belong to an intellectual elite. This is why their attitude towards a new lecturer (myself, for example, when I took up my post) is nothing like that of students from other countries, who are absolutely petrified on their first day in class and offer their teacher their brightest smiles (and in America, an apple). On my first day as a teacher at Oxford, I felt I was in the presence of a group of world-weary know-it-alls who, mentally sprawling in their chairs, seemed to be saying: "Come on, then, amuse us; let's see if you have anything new to tell us, something we don't know already." The truth is that, as long as you fulfilled that first and most sacred precept (and that of any form of teaching, namely, "to amuse"), Oxford students prove to be as receptive as any others and continue to be among the ablest and most appreciative students any teacher could ask for. Perhaps that is why most of the literature students take up jobs that have nothing to do with their degree, but go into politics or banking, it being a widely held view in English society that anyone who has been exposed to the Oxford method of education is thereby qualified to take on any post of responsibility, even if he spent his university years scanning sonnets by Góngora and being bored to death by Spain's post–Civil War novels.

I spent two years in Oxford as a transient lecturer, but only ten days in Cambridge at a conference on English literature to which I had been invited, and so I cannot judge that town with the same lack of impartiality. At first sight, though, the two places are as alike as two peas in a pod, so much so that this extreme superficial likeness makes one suspect the existence of enormous underlying differences. Nevertheless, it should be said that in Oxford, where one senses an instinctive disdain for graduates from any other university in the world, they treat those who come from Cambridge with an exquisite respect tinged with a deep-seated loathing, as if the Oxonians felt more comfortable with a uniqueness so peculiar that it is best shared between the two of them.

From the point of view of a continental (or, rather, southern European) writer, Oxford seems to be the exact opposite of the university world I have known: the foresight, common sense, acuity, good manners, fabulous libraries, didactic seriousness, irony, centuries-old rituals, respect for the student, scorn for charlatans, and that bunch of keys are precisely the things that Spanish universities lack. Above all else, though, you can find in Oxford something that is most unusual nowadays, not just in my country, but in almost any other: in a university world dominated by resolute mediocrity and a desire to perpetuate it (thus ensuring jobs for life for the mediocrities who have already been enthroned), it is both surprising and stimulating to find a real appreciation of talent, which, miraculously, is not seen as a danger or a threat. Perhaps that is why Oxford is the only place on the planet (bearing in mind that shared uniqueness I mentioned earlier) where, on one afternoon you can go and hear E. H. Gombrich, the following afternoon P. E. Russell, the next Francis Haskell, the next Isaiah Berlin and the next George Steiner. And if you're a visitor, you can do all those things, without crowds and for free.

(1990)

Venice, An Interior

The Venetians

Let us begin with what you don't see, perhaps the only thing that isn't on show, whose existence seems improbable and, to the visitor, almost impossible. People who *live* in Venice! Men and women who have nothing to do with the tourist machine and who live there *permanently*! Human beings who spend the whole year in that Great Museum, throughout the city's four long seasons! Individuals who are not content with the mere three or five or seven days that every mortal should set aside in the vast diary of his or her biography to be spent in the one place in the world that, if left unvisited, could tarnish the worthy portrait of someone who throughout his life—however decent or dissolute—has always done his aesthetic duty!

Only this threat to the perfection of our lived experience can explain why it is that, along with younger tourists (the dreaded backpackers who muddy the waters in summer), vast groups of ancient, even decrepit, visitors appear in St. Mark's Square with eyes protected by cameras with dioptre lenses or else fixed firmly on the ground, as if they were afraid to look up and straight ahead and finally see what it is deemed vital that every human being on the planet should see at least once, as if looking up might bring about their own immediate departure to that other paradise from which there is no return. Indeed, sometimes the crews on the planes that land at Marco Polo Airport—with its distinctly Central American feel—won't allow the able-bodied passengers off for a good half-hour because of the large number of "wheelchairs" (as a stewardess with a utilitarian mindset insists on calling the people occupying them) who have to be deposited on terra firma first and by the not entirely risk-free means of rudimentary cranes and plastic toboggans. An hour later, of course, the "wheelchairs" will have to tackle the insoluble problem of climbing innumerable steps and bridges, but at least they will not have to add to their other misfortunes the ignominy of never having seen Venice. You simply have to see it.

Venetians are aware of this, and the knowledge that their city is the key destination in the rest of humanity's dream geography has forged their character and determined how they view themselves in relation to the world. It's hardly surprising then that Venetians, even now, consider themselves to be the centre of that world so hell-bent on visiting them that it is prepared, if necessary, to do so on its knees. Some of the more arrogant Venetians can still be heard to say that the *campo*—the country—begins on the other side of the Ponte della Libertà, the only connection (apart from the railway bridge) between the mainland and the group of islands that make up the city. That two-mile-long bridge, the brainchild of Mussolini, Vittorio Cini and Count Volpi de Misurata, has attached the city to the peninsula for well over fifty years now, allowing cars to lay siege to Venice, at its very gates, like some new form of dragon, and the bridge is perceived by Venetians as an impertinent umbilical cord, which they have no option but to accept. For Venetians, Venice is the City par excellence. The rest of the world is merely *campo*. The harshest and most belligerent version of this idea has a racist variant: "Blacks begin on the other side of the Ponte della Libertà."

But these inhabitants—the only true Whites in their opinion, the only civilized people in all humanity, which they consider barbarous by comparison—are not easy to spot. Invaded, harassed, plundered, driven out and slowly deprived of their White customs and urban traditions, there are ever fewer of those who stubbornly refuse to give any more ground. Throughout the twentieth century Venetians emigrated in steadily growing numbers to Mestre, which started out as a working-class district a few miles from the city and is now the secret envy of those treacherous Venetians who have grown frail and unsteady on their feet, because it has discotheques, cinemas, young people, department stores, supermarkets, things to do, life. In the days of the Republic, Venice had almost three hundred thousand inhabitants. Now there are only seventy thousand, and the desertions are not over yet.

Venetians are not easy to spot; largely because they don't go out very much. Entrenched behind their watermelon-green shutters, they watch the rest of the world—the periphery of the world—in their pyjamas and via their twenty TV channels. Their indifference and lack of curiosity about anything other than themselves and their ancestors has no equivalent in even the most inward-turning of villages in the northern hemisphere. Venice's three cinemas tend to be languid, half-empty places, as do the Teatro Goldoni, the bars and the streets as darkness falls, the lecture theatres and even the concert halls, although, as I will explain later, these are often the exceptions. Almost nothing will drag Venetians from their houses; almost nothing will shift them from their city. They avoid anywhere that has been developed with tourists in mind or that has in some way been contaminated by tourism, which means nearly everywhere. Their space is shrinking fast, but of course you won't see them sitting on café terraces listening to an anachronistic orchestra (clarinet, violin, double bass, grand piano and accordion) in St. Mark's Square, nor in the nearby restaurants and *trattorie*, nor along the shrill, fairground-like Riva degli Schiavoni facing the lagoon, nor, needless to say, in a gondola. And they will only be seen in the ineluctable Caffè Florian at ungodly hours when any visitors are likely to be sleeping the deep sleep of the exhausted tourist. On the other hand, you might find them in places that seem unalluring to the traveller, but which are the last redoubt of the Venetians' circumscribed habits, places about which travel agents neglect to inform their already overwhelmed clientele: at midday, the Venetian ladies and gentlemen drink their aperitif in Paolin, an unassuming ice-cream parlour-cum-bar; they take their evening stroll along the sublime Zattere; and after dark, night owls and music lovers can be found in the old-fashioned, hidden-away Salone Campiello, one of the few places that stays open after ten o'clock. On opera nights, of course, the locals can be found at the eighteenth-century Teatro La Fenice, the favourite meeting place of the whitest and most urbane of Venetians, that is, the proudest, most exclusive, most scornful and influential. Not that La Fenice is a particularly important theatre, nor can the operatic tradition of Venice be compared with that of Milan, but it is there, in the orchestra stalls, that the *gente per bene*, the true Venetians, go to see and be seen.

Precisely because the strictly musical function of those seats is even more reduced or attenuated than it is in most such places, they become a showcase for dresses, shoes, fur coats and jewels; and the Venetians' own ignorance of the outside world leads them to misjudge how much to display or, to be more exact, to show no judgement at all. Singers at the theatre sometimes complain that their voices cannot be heard above the rattle of jewellery and that their eyes are dazzled by the glint of gold in the darkness, because some ladies do rather over-adorn hands, ears and neck in their eagerness to outshine, well, themselves principally.

Indeed, that is one of the identifying features of the Venetians, by which I mean their need to get dressed up and put on fine clothes, shoes and jewellery. In fact, the curious traveller will probably be able to identify the few natives he may come across in his wanderings fairly easily because, just as tourists go around looking shabby, not to say downright grubby, Venetians seem always to be on their way to some elegant party at any time of the day or year, even when the heat and humidity join forces to leave the most dapper dripping with sweat. You can recognize Venetian women in particular by three things: their lovely carved, chiselled, angular faces are always heavily made-up like the women in Egon Schiele paintings; they walk very fast; and they have beautiful, toned legs from a lifetime of going up and down steps and crossing bridges.

Nevertheless they're not that easy to spot. They don't even take the same streets as tourists. Driven out of the bright main thoroughfares, where the continuous flow of people occasionally causes human traffic jams that are frustrating in the extreme to those with appointments to keep, Venetians seek out short cuts and set off down byways that no foreigner would venture into for fear of becoming lost forever in the unfathomable labyrinth that is Venice: alleys barely wide enough for one person, narrow passageways between two buildings, arcades that appear to lead nowhere, back lanes that look as if they will end up in the canal. The Venetians have been obliged to surrender their streets to incomers, to people from the *campo*, and they traverse instead a hidden Venice, parallel to that of the tourist itineraries signed with yellow arrows. In fact, they don't often get to enjoy the loveliest parts of their city, the ones that everyone else dreams of seeing: they see instead chipped and crumbling walls, tiny bridges over anonymous dwarfish canals, cracked and peeling stucco, the reverse side of the city, its shadow-self, in which there are no shops or hotels, restaurants or bars, only the essential elements, stone and water. They also avoid the crowded *vaporetti*, or waterbuses, and so are forced to walk miles whenever they leave the house. At most, they might allow themselves to take the *traghetto*, or gondola, which, for a few pence, carries them from one side of the Grand Canal to the other. This, however, also turns out to be one of the city's most thrilling experiences, for while the *traghetto* offers only a brief crossing, avoiding the *vaporetti* and the motorboats travelling up and down the canal, it affords its passengers a glimpse of the palaces from the height at which they were intended to be seen.

The Archipelago

Venetians, as well as those who, though not born in Venice, live here, and, indeed, even those visitors who dare to stay longer than the period stipulated by most conventional biographies, all end up losing the desire or will to leave the city. We can discuss later the real reason for this strange fixity, for the total engagement with the city felt by those who linger too long in Venice, this mixture of contentment and resignation. The fact is, though, that Venetians rarely leave their city, and when they do, it is only in order to travel somewhere that has always belonged to them anyway.

The large island of the Lido, whose beaches Visconti immortalized in that collection of picture postcards for maritime aesthetes entitled *Death in Venice*, is today, in contrast to what we were shown in the film, a totally domestic place, and not in the least international. It's a family beach to which Venetians travel daily during the month of

July, making the twenty-minute crossing over the grey waters of the lagoon. Awaiting them will be a beach hut, which, for the season, will have cost them five million lira to rent, and which they will use for that one month and the first week of September only, because in August they will be holidaying in "their" mountains, the Dolomites. These are probably the greatest distances they will cover in the whole of their reclusive existences. The Venetians' fugitive nature even obliges them to avoid the beach of the Hotel des Bains on which Dirk Bogarde's drowsy eyes lingered so interminably. Not only do they fear that it might attract the occasional tourist made up to look like Aschenbach or coiffed à la Tadzio, they also consider it second-rate. The really good beach, they say, belongs to the Hotel Excelsior.

The Lido, in other respects, is a summer version of the orchestra stalls at La Fenice. Venetian society is so inbred that, just as its members despise all foreigners (not to mention their compatriots, especially if they're *terroni*, people who come from any city south of Rome), they admire each other immensely, and in places where they know that they're likely to meet, they do their utmost to arouse the boundless admiration of their mirror images. This is why the ladies arrive at the beach wearing designer silk dresses, strappy gold stilettos and all the diamonds, emeralds, sapphires, pearls and aquamarines they have at their disposal. The silks and the shoes will be left in the beach hut, but the jewellery and the gold will remain even when the lady decides to take a break from social chit-chat for a moment and bathe in the warm, pale waters of the sea.

Each island in the small archipelago of which Venice forms a part seems to have or have had some specific function. Venice itself is made up of a group of islands and, before it took on the identity of a city, it was called the Rialto. Nowadays, seen from above, there appear to be only two islands, separated by the Grand Canal as if by a pair of meticulous, patient, curved scissors. Put together so that they almost fit each other, the islands look rather like a painter's palette. These two islands are not intended to serve anyone, but to be served by others. Determined that her immutable surface or face should be exposed only to the important things in life, Venice distributes about the lagoon any task or occupation or service that is deemed too specialized or too shameful, anything subsidiary, unpleasant, functional, unsavoury, anything that should not be seen and has no place in the city's administrative, ecclesiastical, courtly, nautical, commercial self.

So, for example, the island of Sant'Erasmo is the city's garden. From there and from the islands of Vignole and Mazzorbo come almost all of Venice's fruit and vegetables. Taking a boat along the canals of Vignole is like plunging into a jungle landscape. The green areas that you don't see in Venice (they do exist, but are hidden) are to be found on these island-gardens, on these island-warehouses. San Clemente and San Servolo, for their part, were home, respectively, to the insane asylums for men and women, until those institutions were abolished by the Italian state ten or fifteen years ago. San Lazzaro degli Armeni was a leper colony until the eighteenth century, when, as its name indicates, it was handed over to the large and highly cultured Armenian community, just as La Giudecca was the island chosen by the Jews (the ghetto was another matter) as a place to live. Sacca Sessola received TB patients, while on San Francesco del Deserto there is only a monastery (Franciscan of course) with immaculately kept gardens patrolled by peacocks. Burano has its speciality too: the famous *merletti*, or lace, although most of what is sold there now is made in Hong Kong and Taiwan—as is almost everything sold anywhere in the world. And Murano, where you can find the astonishing apse of Santa Maria e San Donato, dating from the end of the eleventh century, is, otherwise, a succession of shops and factories making and selling hand-blown glass, the business from which the island makes its living. There they create Barovier fruit, Venini vases and Moretti wine goblets. Indeed, the whole island has a glassy stare to it.

However, the most thrilling of the islands is Torcello. There is almost nothing on Torcello: two churches, three restaurants and La Locanda Cipriani. According to Giovanna Cipriani, the granddaughter of the founder of this exquisite chain of hotels and restaurants, St. Hemingway, the patron saint of tourists, used to stay at La Locanda, existing for days on end on a diet of sandwiches and wine, large quantities of which (the wine) were taken up to him in his room. The rest of the island is barely populated and dominated by some curiously unrampant vegetation.

But Torcello is basically where Venice originated, the first island that looked likely to be inhabited permanently by refugees from Aquileia, Altino, Concordia and Padua, who built stilt-houses in the estuary in their temporary flight from the Barbarian invasions of the fifth century. Torcello was the most important of the islands in those early days, yet now only two churches have been left standing, both of which date from that period. It is a place that has returned to its natural state. The cathedral of Santa Maria Assunta and the small church of Santa Fosca are both unlikely remnants of the Venetian-Byzantine style of the eleventh and twelfth centuries (although the former also contains elements from the seventh century) and of a population that (unlike the Venetians themselves, whose numbers grew and then stopped growing) grew and decayed to the point where the earth swallowed up the palaces and the other churches, the monasteries and the houses, as well as a flourishing wool industry. Venice is not a true ruin, but Torcello is, the victim of its increasingly swampy waters and of malaria. In one of the mosaics inside the cathedral (the one showing the Last Judgement), there is an extraordinary depiction of Lucifer. To his right stand some spear-wielding angels busily flinging into the fires of hell those found guilty of pride, here represented by crowned and mitred heads with ermine collars and bejewelled ears. Those heads are immediately seized upon by small green angels, the fallen ones. Lucifer, seated on a throne the arms of which are the heads of dragons engaged in devouring human bodies, has the same face and is making the same gesture as God the Father; he has the same abundant white beard and hair, the same venerable appearance, his right hand raised in a gesture of greeting and of serenely imposed order. On his knees sits a pretty child all dressed in white, who looks like the Infant Redeemer, God the Son. But Lucifer's face and body are dark green: he is a topsy-turvy version of God the Father, or, rather, a negative version, and the child sitting on his lap is the Antichrist, who also has his right hand raised in greeting—the very same gesture—like a small prince gently beckoning to the dead.

The dead in Venice have their own island too, occupying the whole of San Michele, whose walls—it is the only walled island—can be seen from the *vaporetto* as you approach. The tops of cypresses wave above the walls, warning the visitor of what awaits them. And the view from the water provides the best perspective from which to see the façade of the Renaissance church, built by that excellent architect Codussi, and made, like so many other Venetian churches, out of white Istrian stone, one of the city's colours.

The cemetery of San Michele, though, is an impersonal place. Unlike the cemeteries of Hamburg or Lisbon or Scotland, there are no large groups of monumental sculptures or inspired inscriptions, but merely descriptive notes, firmly rooted in life rather than addressed to the hereafter: "Elizabetta Ranzato Zanon, a woman of strong character," as one can see from the relief carving of her rather grumpy face; "Pietro Giove Fu Antonio, an honest businessman"; "Giuseppe Antonio Leiss di Laimbourg, an expert and disinterested lawyer with a heart of gold." One of the more elegant graves appears to contain the remains of an apocryphal Emily Brontë character: "Gambirasi Heathcliff." As a nod to the tourists, there are arrows on which appear three names: "Stravinsky, Diaghilev, Pound." The first two are in the Greek section, where the composer lies beside his wife, Vera, their identical graves bearing only their names picked out in black-and-blue mosaic. They are very distinguished tombs, rather enviable, made from white marble and edged in red granite. On each tomb lie three withered carnations, which make me think of poor Schubert's possibly fake tomb in Vienna, surrounded now by a garden. Far too many famous people have passed through Venice, and Pound's grave, for example, is now a green mound bearing only his name, lost in the middle of the rarely visited and much neglected evangelical area, where twisted fragments of fallen crosses have impaled the gravestones themselves. It's almost impossible to find Pound's grave among the undergrowth. No one repairs the damage wrought by a recent storm. In the summer, the only visitors to the dead of San Michele are the lizards, no one else. Who in Venice would have time to tend the graves of these foreign dead, of the vanished lives of these visitors? Foreigners die here more definitively. Perhaps that's why they keep coming, to tempt fate.

The Point of View of Eternity

In Venice, perhaps fortunately, there are only one or two paintings by Canaletto. Nearly everything he produced is to be found in

Britain thanks to Consul Joseph (or Giuseppe) Smith (1674–1770), who spent forty-four years in the city before being honoured with that diplomatic title, although, in fact, he brought far more honour to the title than it did to him. As a fabulously wealthy trader in fish and meat and as one of the greatest art collectors of his day, Consul Smith lived for seventy of his ninety-six years in Venice, most of them in the Palazzo Mangilli-Valmarana, on the corner of the Grand Canal and Rio dei Santi Apostoli. He had more than enough time during those seven decades to gather together various collections of paintings, sculptures, musical instruments, scores, manuscripts, books, engravings, coins, cameos, medals and jewels, which he later sold for exorbitant prices to the Crown of England; he also sponsored and promoted many artists, among them the Ricci brothers, Zuccarelli, Rosalba Carriera and, of course, Canaletto. Of the latter's work—and this is why so little of it can be found in Venice—Consul Smith managed to sell virtually everything and even dispatched the painter to work in London for ten years. Every wealthy English visitor wanted to take home some visual souvenir of his stay in the city, and what more appropriate, reliable or exact souvenir could there be than a view by Canaletto? His paintings were the equivalent of postcards for those pioneering tourists, the English aristocrats who always included Venice in their Grand Tour.

But although the present-day visitor will see few Canalettos and will have to make do with reproductions or with memories, he will see many Venetian landscapes from the same period, by Guardi, Marieschi, Carlevaris, Bellotto, Migliara, in the city's various museums. And yet, as I said earlier, perhaps it's fortunate that there are virtually no Canalettos, those precise, detailed, almost photographic records, because the views you get in the paintings of those eighteenth-century *vedutisti* are, astonishingly, exactly the same as those you will see on emerging from the Galleria dell'Accademia or Ca' Rezzonico or Museo Correr. This strange sensation produces an equally strange mixture of euphoria and unease. And the truth is that those feelings are only intensified if you have also seen certain paintings by Gentile Bellini, Mansueti or Carpaccio. For you discover that nothing has changed, not just in two hundred and fifty years, but in almost five hundred. The canvases from the cinquecento will show almost the same views as were painted in the settecento; and in the novecento, you stagger, exhausted, out of the museums, only to be confronted by the same scenes outside. The biggest change will doubtless be the people and their clothes: aristocrats and clerics, black bonnets, long hair, Renaissance cloaks, tight red, white or striped hose in Bellini and Carpaccio; artisans and members of the bourgeoisie, wigs, waistcoats, masks, Saturn hats and loose shirts in Carlevaris or Guardi; crowds of tourists and hideous Bermuda shorts or T-shirts bearing slogans in the streets outside. Everything else, everything nonhuman, remains the same.

The visitor knows this beforehand, and to some degree it is precisely this "archaeological" aspect of the city that has impelled him to travel here. And yet it's still impossible not to be a little surprised when you stop and think about it, or if you try the simple experiment of looking at a couple of paintings and then at your surroundings. Venice is the only city in the world whose past you do not have to glimpse or intuit or guess at, it's there before you, at least its past appearance is, which is also its present appearance. Even more exciting and disquieting is the fact that the city's present appearance is also the city's future appearance. Looking at Venice now, not only do you see it as it was one hundred, two hundred and even five hundred years ago, you see it as it will be in one hundred, two hundred, probably even five hundred years' time. Just as it is the only inhabited place in the world with a visible past, so it is also the only one with its future already on display.

There has been some construction work—a few houses in the more working-class areas, the new headquarters of the Cassa di Risparmio in Campo Manin (the work of the famous architect Pier Luigi Nervi in 1963), the Previdenza Sociale, the Mussolinian railway station and a few others—but, apart from that, you could say that all building ceased in Venice before its current inhabitants were born. And you can, above all, be quite sure that nothing will be built, unless one of the houses were to be destroyed by some unforeseen event, leaving a gap for the architects of the present and the future to fill.

It's rather touching to think that, despite this, Venice has her own twentieth-century architectural genius in Carlo Scarpa (1906–78), who was born here. Scarpa's case is significant though; his wonderful, instantly recognizable works are, in Venice, reduced to mere details, but he is nevertheless revered by his fellow Venetians, who live among the most perfect collection of architectural monuments in history; they go into raptures over the Olivetti Showroom in St. Mark's Square, the doors of the faculties of Architecture or Literature, the old lecture hall (restored by him) in Ca' Foscari, the staircase in Casa Balboni or the courtyard of the Fondazione Querini Stampalia. In each of these, there might be four steps to admire, or a roof or a door or a radiator grille. That is what the work of the great Carlo Scarpa consists of in his native city. No one can touch Venice, and he was no exception. Venice is the city with the clearest idea of its own future, and that is why perhaps the past—the immense, omnipresent, overwhelming weight of the past—is never set against an identical and already known future, but against the threat of disappearance.

Ever since my first visit to Venice in 1984, I have been back twice or more each year. Now, I may be wrong, but I have always had the sense that the threat of catastrophe, of irremediable calamity or total annihilation, was less a genuine fear among its inhabitants and more of a necessity. This deliberate feeling of dread—artificially created, in my view—immediately infects visitors too, probably even the most ephemeral ones, who have only to set foot on a bridge to feel that this could well be the city's final day.

Venice is the most protected and studied city in the world, the most closely monitored and watched. The universal desire is not only to preserve it, but to preserve it exactly as it is now. We know that it cannot cease to exist, that it cannot be lost. Probably not even a world war would permit that. The terrible certainty that something we can actually see will always be there and will always remain the same, without the admixture of unease and uncertainty inherent in all human enterprises and communities, without the possibility of a new life or of an unprecedented rebirth, of growth or expansion, without the possibility, in short, of any surprise or change, means that Venetians see life from "the viewpoint of eternity." That is the phrase used by Mario Perez who, despite his name (without an accent on the first "e"), is one of the few people born, raised and still living in Venice whom it has been my privilege to know. The viewpoint of eternity! The words froze my blood while we were having supper together: I was eating sole, and he salmon. Can there be a more frightening, unbearable, less human point of view?

I suppose the only way of making that certainty and that viewpoint bearable is to give in to the temptation of believing in the imminent destruction of what will doubtless survive us, and to foster the threat and fear of total extinction. Each time I arrive in Venice, I find the population alarmed about something or other, be it an old threat or a new. Sometimes it's stone decay, which is corroding the city faster than in past centuries; sometimes it's the backpackers and the excessive number of *pendolari* (day-trippers, of whom there can be as many as thirty thousand daily); at others it's the *acqua alta*, when the tide is unusually high and overflows into the lower parts of the city (starting with St. Mark's Square), ruining shopkeepers, requiring benches to be put together to form improvised mini-bridges in the streets, and causing terrible flooding, as happened on 4 November 1966, that disastrous day when the water rose more than six feet, leaving everything stained with damp and caked in salt for months afterwards; the city is, of course, slowly sinking, at the rate of about six inches a century, they say; the nearby industries have succeeded in corroding the stone in only a matter of years, far more quickly than in any of the previous, far less productive centuries; and there is always the possibility that an earthquake might transform Venice into a vast, labyrinthine underwater palace (years ago, minor tremors caused some of the smaller islands in the lagoon to vanish).

One of the more recent threats has been the proliferation of algae in the bottom of the lagoon, together with a plague of Chironomidae, insects that resemble clumsy mosquitoes and sometimes form such dense clouds that they blacken windows or force trains to stop and planes to abandon take-off. The detritus from the factories in neighbouring Marghera acts like a fertilizer on the algae, which grow and reproduce so fast that four boats scooping up thousands of tons of the stuff day and night haven't been enough to clear the lagoon bed. The algae rot in the boiling summer heat. The fish die and float on the surface as if they were the water's unexpected, multiple gaze. And depending which way the wind is blowing (or even if there is no wind at all), a smell of pestilence takes over the city. It's the all-enveloping stench of putrefaction. The fetid odour wakes you in the middle of the night, and whereas in any other place this would be assumed to be a temporary phenomenon, in Venice, you somehow imagine it will be perpetual, global, a state of mind, a clear sign that the end of civilization is nigh. These perhaps are the disadvantages of living life from the viewpoint of eternity.

The Night Stroll

Apart from going to see the things you feel obliged to see and which are never-ending, the only diversion in Venice in August is to walk and look and walk and look. Not that there's very much more to do in winter, apart, now and then, from the occasional concert or, under the auspices of Agnelli, a new exhibition hung on the pink-tinged walls of Palazzo Grassi. In fact, the only thing Venetians have in common with their former invaders, the Austrians, is their passion for music. Concerts are the one event for which you cannot find tickets, and among the few moments that remain fixed in the homogenizing memory of Venice's inhabitants is the night, for example, when the pianist Sviatoslav Richter stopped time (and this in a place where time stands still anyway) with the second movement of a Haydn sonata at La Fenice. But then, in August, everything grinds to a halt, and for those citizens and tourists who don't want to see one of the films being shown on the giant open-air screen erected in Campo San Polo and who aren't too worn out by their daytime wanderings, by the heat or by Stendhal syndrome—which claims many victims here—their only option will be to walk and look.

The city changes completely at night. It's one of the liveliest cities I know during the day, but when the sun sets, everything disappears or closes, and as the hours pass, Venice becomes ever more deserted and ever more the province of individual noises. The sound of footsteps is intercut with the slap of water, and almost any corner of the city looks even more like a stage set than usual, given that a set never looks quite so set-like as when it's empty. But what really changes Venice is the darkness itself. At night—this is the complaint of many of the biblical hordes of tourists—it's barely lit at all, apart from the occasional church or palace on the Grand Canal. Along the minor canals and backstreets, which constitute the real city, there is only perhaps a street lamp here, a lantern there, the occasional miserly crack of light between those watermelon-green shutters. There are places where the darkness is almost total, and you can stand on a bridge for hours vainly trying to make out anything more than the mere outline of buildings and the invisible flow of water. Water is the city's fundamental element. By day, it reflects and intensifies the light and colour (blood red, yellow, white) of the houses and the palaces. By night, though, it reflects nothing. It absorbs. On moonless nights—last night, for example—it's like ink, and so seems much more stagnant than it actually is. Then the only real illumination comes from the buildings made of that intensely white Istrian stone: Santa Maria della Salute or the Palazzo Mocenigo Casa Nuova; San Giorgio Maggiore or Il Redentore, seen from the Zattere.

The walker who fears getting lost in the gloomier corners of the city, but fancies a lengthy stroll along a spacious promenade by the water, has two options: Riva degli Schiavoni or the Zattere. The first, which begins at St. Mark's Square, will be popular with those who require some continuity of appearance between different places.

There, on Schiavoni, they will still find people, possibly too many: the hustle and bustle of street-sellers, crowds of young people, Japanese and Spanish, standing around the obelisks, restaurants and bars, although few of the latter will remain open past midnight. The extremely bronzed waiter at the Bar do Leoni, who was filing his nails at midafternoon in readiness to welcome customers exhausted by fatigue and ecstasy, will already be putting the chairs back on the tables. A little further east, the endless lines of moored *motoscafi* are rocked by the coming and going of the lagoon waters, producing, as they do, an extraordinary symphony of metallic squeaks and bumps that must be a torment to the inhabitants of the old people's home opposite. There are still crowds on Riva degli Schiavoni, but they are a spent force. Only Harry's Bar, a short distance in the opposite direction, will proudly continue to be full of life, with its gallery of well-dressed characters and its American families following in the footsteps of the blessed Hemingway. Its small legendary dining room, preserved intact since 1931 by the Cipriani family, is definitely the best restaurant in the city, and a meal there is something that should be afforded even by those who really can't.

But the other long *fondamenta*, or walkway, that takes you past broad stretches of water (in the Grand Canal there are only short sections that are passable) is the so-called Zattere (meaning, literally, rafts). The Zattere runs along the southernmost edge of the city, from which you can contemplate the island of La Giudecca, separated from Venice proper by a wide canal of the same name, so wide and deep that ships sail down it. The extraordinary Fondamenta delle Zattere is well known but somewhat hidden and will be found only by those, for example, who, after visiting the church of Santa Maria della Salute, go as far as the end of the Dogana, the old Customs House, and then turn back on themselves. Unlike the Riva degli Schiavoni, it is silent and fairly solitary. Now and then you might encounter a café terrace where a few of the city's inhabitants and a handful of well-informed visitors are enjoying a quiet drink or an ice cream, but otherwise there are only long stretches of stone pavement, to one side of which is a wall and to the other water, although the wall is now and then interrupted by a low bridge beneath which flows a *rio*, or minor canal, pointing the way back into the heart of Venice.

On the other side of the Canale della Giudecca, you can see the island, with the Palladian Chiesa del Redentore lit up, and further east, greatly foreshortened, on its own island, the church of San Giorgio Maggiore, also designed by Palladio. The walker must then turn his back on that and start crossing bridges: Ponte dell'Umiltà, Ponte Ca' Balà, Ponte agli Incurabili. The only thing approaching a crowd you are likely to meet is a couple who have perhaps reached the Zattere by chance or on a whim and are standing on a bridge, unsure which way to go next, or perhaps watching one of the big ships passing, and which has suddenly become a moving part of La Giudecca. Since both buildings and ships in Venice are on a level with the water, and since the buildings are never more than two or three or four storeys at most, they can easily disappear behind a large vessel, and there are moments when a Russian or Dutch or Greek ship completely supplants the Chiesa del Redentore or Chiesa delle Zitelle, as if in a scene from a Hitchcock film, erasing them from our vision for a few seconds. You come across children too, fishing for squid and plaice with nets. "*Una seppia e sette passarini*," says one small bespectacled child, when I ask him what's in his plastic bag. Meanwhile, a lizard escapes along the wall to my right. After the next bridge, della Calcina, there is a plaque commemorating John Ruskin, "the high priest of art," to whom, according to the inscription, "every marble, every bronze, every painting, every thing cried out." This inconsiderate cacophony might go some way to explaining the more hysterical passages in that high priest's *Stones of Venice*.

Further on, past the Ponte Lungo and towards the west, as you approach the Stazione Marittima and the end of the Zattere and the walk itself, you see the most amazing sight of all. During the day, to the west, you can make out the industrial complexes of neighbouring Marghera, but what we're interested in lies straight ahead, where La Giudecca ends. Looming out of the darkness on the other side stand two buildings of a Nordic or Hanseatic appearance; they are tall and square and one of them is a colossal seven storeys high, something you never see in Venice. The larger of the two is a colourless hulk. Shortly before you reach them, the waters of La Giudecca are still reflecting the bright lamps outside Harry's Dolci, another establishment belonging to the Cipriani empire. There, however, beneath those Nordic hulks—like a chunk of Hamburg or Copenhagen—the water is blacker than at any other point, there's not even a security guard's flashlight or a light left on by some insomniac. There are no Gothic windows, no Renaissance mouldings, no white Istrian stone, not a trace of red, just a dark, gloomy, derelict, nineteenth-century construction: this is Molino Stucky, the vast flour factory erected in 1884 despite many protests, and which has stood empty since the Second World War. So far, no new purpose has been found for it that would justify its restoration, its return to life. The waiter in the restaurant opposite eyes these "modern" buildings scornfully and tells me that they're completely deserted apart from "*pantegane come gatti*" (which means "rats as big as cats"). This mass of iron, brick and slate, the one factory to be built within the city's confines, rises up, decayed and austere, like a trophy won by Venice itself, that paradise of the unnecessary and the useless, with its back turned haughtily on the present. Everything unnecessary and useless, everything that can only be walked past and looked at, remains alive, sometimes escaping ruin by a hair's breadth. In the unnecessary and useless there is always a light, however faint, even if its sole purpose is to illuminate the surrounding gloom, as Faulkner once said about striking a match in the darkness. Molino Stucky, however, lies in permanent darkness, and the walker along the Zattere, across the water, will struggle to guess the past of that emblematic tower and pinnacle, those futile walls and blind windows, a far less distant, but less decipherable, past than that of any palazzo.

The Imaginary Space

You could walk from the west to the east of Venice (which is the longest possible distance) in about an hour, at a brisk pace and without getting out of breath. But almost no one does this: firstly, because it's difficult, if not impossible, to follow a relatively straight line without pausing a hundred times en route; and, secondly, because of what we, rather pedantically, might call its "endless imaginary fragmentation."

Venice provokes two simultaneous and apparently contradictory feelings: on the one hand, it is the most homogeneous—or, if you prefer, harmonious—city I have known. By homogeneous or harmonious I mean that any point in the city that enters the observer's field of vision, any luminous open space or secret misty corner, with water or without, could only possibly belong to this one city, could never be confused with any other urban landscape or evoke memories of elsewhere; it is, therefore, the very opposite of anodyne. (With the possible exception of Lista di Spagna, that stretch of street which, to the great confusion and misfortune of many visitors arriving by train, is the first thing one sees; it is best, therefore, to jump on a *vaporetto* or immediately cross the bridge.)

On the other hand (and herein lies the contradiction), few cities seem more spread out and more fragmented, full of insuperable distances and places that feel utterly isolated. Venice is divided into six *sestieri*, or quarters: San Marco, San Polo, Cannaregio, Santa Croce, Dorsoduro and Castello. Even within each *sestiere* there are areas that seem a world away from any other, even the world that is not only next door, but adjacent and contiguous.

This feeling is not entirely false, insofar as it's not exclusive to the visitor, who, unfamiliar with the city's meandering streets, might miscalculate and think that he set off from his starting point earlier than he actually did; rather, it has deep roots in the inhabitants of Venice themselves, and I am not referring, as I did earlier, only to the most powerful, to the movers and shakers (although never have I known movers and shakers move or shake less), but to the ordinary inhabitants, shopkeepers, the few remaining craftsmen, housewives, and, of course, children, who, here as elsewhere—unlikely as it may seem—have to go to school. Mario Perez tells me that he knows a lady who, like him, lives in Castello, but who has never once set foot in St. Mark's Square; now and then she asks him how things are going over there in the same tone of voice in which she might inquire about events in Madagascar or some other remote place from which he had just returned after a long voyage, bearing fresh news. This "imaginary" distancing is a condition of existence in Venice: you live mainly in the restricted world of the street, the canal or the quarter, and the totality of Venice (and therein lies its harmony and homogeneity) is perceived only in fragments, albeit perfectly articulated. The Venetians are, of course, the ones most keenly aware of this fragmentation and articulation, but the astonishing thing is that, intuitively and possibly with no need for it to be put into words, this awareness instantly takes root in visitors as well, however transient and unobservant they may be. And it is doubtless this intuited notion that forbids them—if I may put it so—from entering many parts of the city, into which they will never venture even if the map is telling them that they are only a step away.

Perhaps they're right not to take risks. The more adventurous visitor might reach Campo dell'Anconetta heading towards Strada Nova, very close to the Grand Canal, which will always serve him as the city's axis. Suddenly, seduced by curiosity or by the desire to see a particular church, he might turn left and cross no fewer than three canals—Rio della Misericordia, Rio della Sensa, Rio della Madonna dell'Orto—and find himself in front of the superb church bearing the latter name. And the five minutes it took him to get there might be enough to give him the strange impression that he is a thousand leagues from the Grand Canal. Having studied the ten Tintorettos in that church and the beautiful Bellini Virgin depicting a lunatic Christ Child who looks as if he's either going to choke to death at any moment or pounce on his extraordinary mother, the visitor will doubtless retrace his steps and be astonished to find how close he was to something that was clearly far away while he was wandering beside those secondary canals, because he really *was* far away.

Space in Venice should be measured by state of mind and character and by the *idea* that emanates from each *sestiere*, each quarter, each canal and each street, not by the number of yards separating them. For example, the same person seen in different places will vary, even though his function or activity is the same in all of them. There is in Venice a beggar (oddly enough, despite all those tourists, you don't see many, which is why they're easy to recognize) who begs for alms in all six *sestieri*. He's rather chubby and getting on in years; he wears a hat that is a tad too small for him, plays the pan-pipes—an instrument that betrays his southern origins—and displays to the compassionate gaze of passers-by a pale, plump plastic calf that emerges from a very short white sock. It is the cleanest leg I have ever seen, and I always stop to look at it. I give him a few coins to reward such cleanliness as well as the pleasant sound of his pipes. This eminently recognizable man, however, is quite different depending on whether he's in San Marco, San Polo, Cannaregio, Santa Croce, Dorsoduro or Castello. In the first of those *sestieri*, he seems like a fraud or a local con man preying on tourists; in the second, his "foreign" *terrone* aspect seems more pronounced and he looks out of place; in the third, he blends in so well that no one even notices that he's begging for alms with his impeccable leg. It's the setting that dictates how things appear, and so it isn't the same seeing a tourist crossing the Rialto Bridge as it is seeing him crossing one of the various Ponti delle Tette. These are the darkest and most hidden, the least touristy of bridges, offering the most limited views, and their name arises from the fact that they were the only bridges on which the Doge would allow the impoverished streetwalkers of the eighteenth century to show their tits—or *tette*—to the passers-by and thus attract more clients, who were apparently too distracted at the time by the exquisite courtesans arriving from all over Europe and by a prevailing fashion for homosexuality.

In Venice, though, each fragment is a whole. Sometimes the streets are so narrow and tortuous that we can see very little, yet a fragment, any fragment, will form a momentary whole, and will be unmistakably Venice. There is nothing more instantly identifiable or more complete than the little San Trovaso *squero*, or dry dock, for gondolas, a tiny wooden construction (wood for once, not stone) next to which a few vessels lie waiting in the dark to be repaired: for the gondolas, which, as I mentioned before, are the perfect height from which to view the city (even the *vaporetti* are too high in the water), continue to have a function and a life and can still be restored, unlike the Molino Stucky. From an arcade behind La Fenice, you can see the glaucous waters of the Rio Menùo, a scrap of pink palace, a large door painted in the usual watermelon green, and a few steps. From where I am writing, I can see the pillars of my balcony, the Rio delle Muneghette, two boats, the shop selling toy windmills, and the Scuola di San Rocco in the background. There are people who will have spent a lifetime seeing only the San Trovaso dock or that fragment of the Rio Menùo or this view from my terrace, just as the old lady in Castello, whom Mario Perez told me about, hasn't once set foot in St. Mark's Square.

Venice is a *hypercity*. Perhaps the smug Venetians who insist that everything else is mere *campo* are, after all, right. There are no exteriors, here everything is stone, everything is built, the gardens you can see from the top of the Campanile are nowhere to be found when you wander through Venice: they are private, enclosed, and belong neither to the walker nor to the general population. Yet there need be nothing artificial about one's relationship with this place of stone, as the panicky, harassed tourists believe, who mistakenly travel here in an exclusively cultural spirit. When I call Venice a *hypercity* or, as Venetians would have it, the City par excellence, I mean, above all, that in the minds of the people who love it, it is those things necessarily and naturally, and perhaps not as deeply cultured as you might think, but at once instinctive and not in the least accidental. A city like this can be natural without, at the same time, owing anything to chance. Perhaps there is another way of understanding and describing it. According to Daniella Pittarello, an Italian from Padua who has lived here for ten years: "Venice is an interior." And she adds that it is precisely because there is no *outside* and because it is complete in itself, that it can be so difficult, albeit necessary some-times, to leave, just as it gets harder and harder to leave home when you haven't done so for a long time. Henry James saw it in a very similar way: "where voices sound as in the corridors of a house, where the human step circulates as if it skirted the angles of furniture and shoes never wear out . . ." To say that Venice is an interior is a possible summation of everything I have said so far. It means that it is self-sufficient, that it has no need of anything outside itself and that this same self-sufficiency is what creates that "endless imaginary fragmentation": the narrow becomes wide, the near becomes far, the limited becomes infinite, the identical becomes distinct, the timeless becomes transient.

The Things We Carry with Us

Between December 1984 and October 1989—for personal reasons I need not go into here—I flew to Venice fourteen times, from Spain and from England and, on one occasion, from the United States. My stays in the city varied in length from the hectic four days of my first visit to the seventy days of my longest visit; and during that five-year period, I spent, in all, a total of nine months in Venice, long enough for me to feel it was a place in which I partially lived, my second—ever-present—city, to which I went and from which I returned, and to which I always thought I would go back. There I wrote a good part of my novels *The Man of Feeling* and *All Souls*, and my day-to-day Venetian life was nothing like that of a tourist, or even of a traveller. I fitted into the routine of the people who so generously took me in, two women, both called Daniela, who shared a house. In order to distinguish them, I would address one as Daniela plus her surname and the other as Daniella, with two "l"s. Since they both worked and had to go out early and I had more time at my disposal, I was left in charge of washing the dishes (rather inexpertly), doing the shopping and running various other domestic errands. Indeed, I had time enough to write those two novels and to stroll about the city on my own, always aimlessly, slowly, calmly, just seeing what I might come across, without any of the haste of normal visitors and the programme of visits they set themselves when they have only a few days in which to get to know a city. At one point, I came very close to settling down there, and had even found myself a job. I didn't know that my fourteenth visit would be my last, or, rather, I didn't know that twenty years would pass before my next visit.

When you have lived for a while in a city, especially if it has proved to be an intense experience and happens to coincide with one of those ages so crucial in most people's lives (between the ages of thirty-three and thirty-eight in my case), regardless of how much time passes, you never stop thinking about that place. You carry it around with you, it becomes part of you, and I often have the strange feeling that I could leave my apartment in Madrid, or anywhere else, and head straight for some particular spot in that distant city, to a church, a shop, a square, to the Zattere or San Trovaso if it's Venice, to St. Giles or Blackwell's if it's Oxford, or to Cecil Court or Glouces-ter Road if it's London. It didn't feel as if twenty years had passed since my last stay there, and yet they had, almost half a lifetime, if you like. We live in a reality that is very different from the past and we certainly don't lose touch with that reality when we receive a sudden visitation from the distant past. However, as I've often said before, space is the only true repository of time, of past time. And that is why, when you go back to a familiar city, time undergoes a brief, sudden compression, and what was far away in Madrid the day before yesterday becomes spuriously close in Venice today. After a first few hesitant steps, those same steps automatically take you along routes you had apparently forgotten the day before, and which you suddenly remember. Almost without thinking, you say: you have to go down there to reach such-and-such a place and to reach so-and-so you head in that direction, and you never get lost or go wrong. There, before me, was the house to which I once had the key, the address was San Polo 3089; I can't go in there now, not just because I no longer have a key, but because the two Danielas no longer live there. Sitting on the steps that separate the water—Rio delle Muneghette—from the back of the Scuola di San Rocco that I used to see from the balcony where I would stand when taking a break from writing those two, now old, novels, I smoke a cigarette and look across at the house and that balcony. The house used to be white, but its new owners have painted it an orangey-pink colour, yet I say to myself: that's the house, I'm sure of it, I spent many an evening and afternoon there; on many nights, I slept there; I would get up in the morning and look out at the water and at the steps on which I'm sitting now, twenty years later.

Fortunately, Venice is barely allowed to change at all, and the barges full of fruit are still there next to Campo San Barnaba, where I would do my somewhat clumsy food-shopping; the church of Santi Giovanni e Paolo is still there, in a square scorned by tourists and which, in any other city, would be its crowded centre. And, to my great good fortune, the people are still there too, and I've made my peace with them. I had supper one night with the two Danielas and with Cristina; they had barely changed, as if they had made a pact with some minor, rather inoffensive devil. Suddenly, in their company, it wasn't that time hadn't passed for each of us (far from it: they've all been married, one is divorced and the other is in the process of getting divorced, one has daughters, another moved to Florence, but came back to Venice especially to see me), but our talk and our laughter were, implausibly, just the same, at least for a while, as it used to be when we were young. It's always very cheering to find there are people and places that are always there, even though they're far away or seem to have been lost. We probably only really lose what we forget or reject, what we prefer to erase and no longer wish to carry with us, what is no longer part of the life we tell ourselves.

Author's Note

Though it is said in this text that Venice never changes, that is inaccurate of course, as all places suffer some changes, even if slight ones. It must be noted that *Venice, An Interior* was written in 1988, when, to give just an example, Molino Stucky was the derelict building here alluded to, and not the present-day hotel it has become. Also, at the time this was written, the interior walls of Palazzo Grassi were painted a shade of pink.

ALL TOO FEW

Noises in the Night

I sometimes wish I were slightly harder of hearing, so that I didn't have to suffer quite so much from the degree of "noise pollution" that exists here in Spain and which is exceeded only by the levels reached in Japan. I'm referring to the strange noises that are made, it would seem, by *all* neighbours, but especially by those who live in the apartments above us when they get home at night.

In fact, I know of no one who has not, at some point in his life, in some apartment he's lived in, come to the conclusion that the upstairs neighbours are in the habit of dragging their furniture about in the wee hours or simply moving it around (beds included), and not just on one night, but almost every night. I'm sure you've had the same incomprehensible feeling. Are they so dissatisfied and uncertain about the position of their furniture that they have to experiment constantly, with the sofa here and the wardrobe over there, the armchairs in that corner and the tables over by the window? Now, there may well be a large number of individuals who really are in a state of hopeless in-decision as to how best to furnish their bedrooms and living rooms, but it's entirely impossible that there are so many of them that we've all had to put up with at least one. So what *is* going on? What unfath-omable things do people get up to late at night, especially those who have to rise early to go to work or to take their children to school, and who do not appear to be remotely bohemian?

If one had to deduce their nocturnal lives from the noises they make, one would conjure up the most bizarre images. I've lived in apartments where I became convinced that my upstairs neighbours, at some late hour of the night, started playing marbles or perhaps pétanque, because the sounds that reached me were unmistakably those of balls rolling across the parquet. With others, it seemed to me that, as soon as they arrived home, all their buttons immediately fell off and dropped to the floor, or that the pearl necklaces they were wearing suddenly broke, which, given the repetitive nature of the noise, led me to conclude that husband and wife must be mutually and respectively wrenching them off, possibly as some kind of fore-play. In an English apartment (appropriately enough) where I stayed for a month, I had the impression that I must be living underneath the little old ladies from Capra's black comedy *Arsenic and Old Lace*, except that instead of killing their victims silently with poison, as the little old ladies did, the tenants evidently spent all night dismember-ing that day's corpse, such was the sound of laborious sawing that came from above. Another time, I came to believe that an elderly man, shy and solitary, was in the habit, as darkness fell, of throwing large, multitudinous parties, given the bustle of footsteps (some even sounded like dance steps) that I could hear from below; this proved not to be the case, because when I did finally give in to the need to satisfy my curiosity and keep watch on the street door from my bal-cony, I saw not a single stranger pass—that is, not a single likely guest; this, however, did not prevent me from hearing them up above, as if they were dancing without music or else chasing each other round the room. For years, a female friend of mine had a neighbour who, as far as she was aware, always entered and left her apartment wearing sensible flat shoes; when her neighbour was at home, however, the noise made by her footsteps convinced my friend that this neighbour must immediately put on a pair of high-heeled mules, to which my friend's imagination couldn't resist adding a couple of pompoms to complete the image: in the end, she was utterly convinced that, each night, her discreet, sober neighbour made up for all that sober discretion by donning a negligee, the aforementioned high-heeled, pompommed mules and, possibly, some sort of diabolical underwear, even if she wasn't expecting a visitor. I once asked some young people about the dull, continuous "papapam" emanating from their apartment, as if they were working some kind of printing press, and their answer was even more bizarre than my imagined explanation: "Oh, we're running an illegal whisky distillery," they told me.

I've found out more over the years: what we take to be the sound of lunatic furniture-shifting is sometimes merely a little rough, extemporaneous vacuuming or even a feverish opening and closing of drawers. On the other hand, one cannot help wondering why people would be opening and closing drawers in the small hours, not just once or twice, but twenty times, or why they would keep banging about with some ancient, metal vacuum cleaner. Of course, in Spain, where almost no one shows any consideration for anyone, there's nothing odd about hearing hammer blows in the middle of the night: it's someone hanging pictures or doing minor home repairs. However, having grown accustomed over the years to hearing so many inexplicable noises, one can't help thinking that the upstairs neighbours are, in fact, hammering nails into a coffin, and one is left with the thought: "I just hope it's theirs."

(2006)

The Modest Case of the
Dead Stork

From the balcony of the apartment that I rent in Soria you can usually
see two storks' nests—at the times of year, of course, when the birds
are present in the city: one on the belfry of the church of San Francisco, the other on the much smaller belfry of the Ermita de la
Soledad, in the lovely park known as La Dehesa. Sometimes you can
see a third nest, built on the top of a tall tree in that same park and
which is, therefore, rather less stable than the first two. The person
who keeps me informed of all this, and about the exploits of the
respective families, is Carme, who is normally terrified of any fea-
thered creature that comes anywhere near her—she has a particular
loathing for pigeons, those vile, winged rats that get such absurdly
good press. However, she does enjoy watching birds from a distance,
through a telescope she brought with her for the purpose, especially
the storks on the nearer nests, who are now part of the landscape, not
to say—absurd expression—part of the family. Her interest in them
has even led her to buy and read a few books about storks, and whenever she takes a break from her work, she always checks on them to
see how they're getting on and at what point they are in their cycle:
if they're still waiting for their mate, if they're building the nest or
incubating, if their chicks have already been born, if they're feeding
them or giving them their first flying lessons.

When I got to the apartment on 2 August, after a month and a half away, Carme had already arrived from Barcelona a few hours before. I had noticed a strange, rank smell as I came up the stairs, and I mentioned this as soon as I saw her. "You're not going to believe it when you see what it is," she said, and led me to the window that opens on to the small inner courtyard, three feet by six or less. There lay a dead stork, where it must have lain for who knows how many days or weeks. It was doubtless a fairly young stork, but it had a really wide wingspan, for the chicks quickly grow to adult size. Anyway, it wasn't just a sparrow or one of those disgusting pigeons or a nice magpie or a noisy blackbird that we—or, rather, I—could easily have picked up. The creature, we assumed, must have had the misfortune to fall when out on a trial flight, and the even worse misfortune to have fallen into our tiny courtyard, from which it would have been unable to escape, and at a time when there was no one in the apartment to lend it a hand. The many white droppings scattered around indicated that the poor thing did not die on impact. What should we do? How were we to get it out of there? Where could we deposit the corpse?

Since our local firemen usually inspire a degree of confidence, I decided to call them. I explained the situation to the person who answered the phone, and he immediately asked: "Is the stork alive?" "No," I said, somewhat taken aback, "I just told you, it's been dead for a while." Then I realized that this absurd question was a way of washing his hands of the affair. "In that case, it's nothing to do with us. If it was wounded, yes, we'd try and rescue it, but if it's dead, then we won't touch it." "Who should I go to for help, then?" I asked. "No idea." Next, I tried the municipal police, some of whose officers are, in my experience, very pleasant, while others are definitely not. The person who answered turned out to belong to the latter contingent. "Is the stork on a public highway?" was his surprising question. "No, as I said, it's in the inner courtyard of our apartment." "Oh, well, if it's inside a building, that's nothing to do with us. If it was out in the street, yes, we'd come and pick it up." And when I asked him whom I should approach, his answer was even more shocking than the fireman's: "I've no idea. You'd better just pick it up yourselves, stick it in a bag and throw it in the bin."

Fortunately, we didn't follow his advice. We tried the Civil Defence, who passed us on to the Civil Guard, who, in turn, put us through to Semprona, the Nature Protection Service. I think I began thus: "I'm not phoning about a live stork or about one that's lying dead in the street, both of which, it seems, have people willing to take care of them, but about one whose corpse is in my apartment . . ." The Semprona people behaved like perfect gentlemen and, the following morning, one of their agents duly arrived to take away the unfortunate beast (this required two enormous plastic bags, out of which poked the bird's beak and feet). Since the stork is a protected species, he questioned us closely, asking: "Are you sure it was already dead when you found it?" That afternoon, the caretaker kindly came up and disinfected the courtyard, which was full of flies, and when we told him what had happened, he said: "You were quite right to ignore the policeman's advice. If you'd been spotted by the police leaving the building carrying two great bags out to the dustbin, with a beak and legs sticking out, they would immediately have assumed you'd killed the bird and promptly arrested you." No wonder the man at Semprona to whom I spoke on the phone had asked me the following touching question, even though he knew from the start that the bird was dead: "Fine, now can you tell me the stork's address?" Just as if the stork were a person—and a permanent resident too.

(2010)

Lady with Bombs

By the time you read these words, the Madrid Book Fair will be over, but I'm writing before it has even begun, and my one wish for the book-signing sessions is that they should be more like the ones I first attended, more than thirty-nine years ago, when I was not yet twenty. Well, at least in one respect. Then, nearly four decades ago, I signed very few books, and most of those were for the relatives and friends who were kind enough to visit the stand, and the truth is that there's something rather embarrassing and sad about sitting there, twiddling your thumbs and desperately trying to look as if you really didn't care that so few people are buying your book. What bothers me now are the manners and attitudes of some of the people who stand in line to get a book signed, although I realize that the more people there are, the more likelihood there is of encountering some troublesome, arbitrary, rude individual. So perhaps I shouldn't complain.

It is nonetheless true that nowadays, as in other areas of public life, one does tend to come across some very touchy, even aggressive, people. There have always been eccentric readers, and I've occasionally been asked to sign not one of my own books (which are the only ones I have the right or the desire to sign), but some classic text that I admire—by Stevenson or Conrad, Dumas or Shakespeare—or by a writer who happens to be a friend. At the recent book fair in

Barcelona, for example, I found myself signing copies of my father's memoirs, as well as *Pomponio Flato* by Eduardo Mendoza and *The Siege* by Arturo Pérez-Reverte. I didn't even object to making my mark, with an indelible felt-tip pen, on someone's e-book holder, which the owner will doubtless curse in future, when he sees the same name appearing over and over, regardless of what he's reading on the wretched gadget, until, of course, he replaces it with another more advanced model, doubtless in the next six months to a year. Such whimsical requests are fairly acceptable, others less so, especially when accompanied by nastiness and rudeness.

Once, again at the book fair in Barcelona, a woman handed me a rose with a piece of paper wrapped round the stem. The paper contained a string of insults, which the donor, doubtless to her great satisfaction, watched me read. Last year, in Madrid, another, rather "striking" woman appeared, striking in the sense that she was well dressed (as regards how much her clothes must have cost, rather than in the sense she intended), relatively young and quite good-looking (although not as good-looking as she thought she was). She took a thick book out of her bag and said: "I'd like you to sign this." I looked at the spine and saw that it was a copy of the Bible. I said: "I'm sorry, I only sign books in which I've been personally involved, be it as author, translator or publisher, although even in the latter case, I prefer not to." "And are you sure you're not personally involved with this one? I think you are," she insisted. "No, I'm quite sure. I would have been pleased to have written certain parts of it or to have witnessed some of the episodes it describes, but, believe me, I had nothing whatsoever to do with it." "Not even in attacking it?" I began to see where she was going with this. "I doubt that anyone could ever inflict much harm on such an enduring work," I replied. She set aside the weighty tome and removed from her purse a small box, only slightly larger than a matchbox. She was clearly well prepared, armed and equipped. "Would you sign this for me, then?" I took a closer look and read on the lid the words: "Stink bombs." You have to remain calm at a book fair, where your role is really almost that of a sales clerk. "I'm sorry, but I had nothing to do with making these either. As I said, I only sign things for which I am responsible." "But you throw stink bombs every week." I assumed she was referring to this column, and one has to accept criticisms, favourable or otherwise. "Well, that depends on one's sense of smell. But, as I say, I had no part in making this little box." She then leaned her elbows on my pile of books, thus blocking the way for all the other people waiting in line, and declared: "I'm not moving from here until you sign that box and the Bible." "Well, you're in for a long wait, then," I said, with ill-disguised irritation now, "because I'm not going to sign either of them."

Eventually, she was gently removed by the very patient bookseller, Javier, and a few "heavies" who turned up when they noticed she was making a scene. When she was some distance away, and while I was dealing with other readers, I noticed that some policemen were asking to see her ID card and I heard her shouting. "You're asking *me* for *my* ID, rather than that gentleman over there!" she yelled, pointing at me. "That man's a political agitator!" When I left, an hour or so later, she was still there, still shouting. At least she didn't let off her stink bombs at the fair. Let's hope she doesn't turn up again this year, even better equipped. The way things are going in this country, any public appearance carries with it a slight risk. Even for writers. Even if it's only a risk to one's olfactory glands.

(2010)

A Horrific Nightmare

After the killing of thirty-two people at Virginia Tech, in a town ominously named Blacksburg, by one mad-as-hell megalomaniac in possession of a private arsenal, the only way that we Europeans can get some idea of the dangers that daily await each citizen of the United States is to imagine a scenario where U.S. rules governing the purchase and possession of firearms also applied on this side of the Atlantic and that, as in America, 40 percent of all households would have at least one weapon, one in four households would keep a pistol in a drawer, and it would be considered perfectly normal for one in three Europeans to be armed. If we focus on Spain alone, this would mean that if the largest superpower has 270 million inhabitants and about 190 million deadly weapons in private hands, here the number of weapons would be around 32 million.

You have to imagine, too, that not a few of these fortunate owners would routinely carry their small arms with them, in their raincoat pocket, in the glove compartment of the car, or in a holster under their arm. Needless to say, any unjustified use of the weapon would be properly punished, as it is in the United States. The problem is that, however hard they came down on the madman who fired without due motive, in the heat of the moment or in a fit of passion, the shots would already have been fired, the bullets would have penetrated, causing irreversible damage, with the dead person dead and no one able to bring him or her back to life. You would also have to imagine that, as is the case in the state of Virginia and in a few other states, almost the only limitation on buying a firearm (apart from the odd little thing like having to prove that you have a clean police record) would be that at least one month must pass between purchases. So each citizen could buy a maximum of *twelve new* weapons a year, which means that, after a period of five years, a keen marksman would have *only sixty* weapons. "Hey," the guy would say, "it's the first of the month, I'm going to get me that grenade-launcher I need."

You have to imagine, therefore, that in this frequently ill-tempered country of ours, the driver boxed in by someone else's double-parking and who passes the time honking his horn and annoying the whole neighbourhood could just as easily resort to gunshots, as could the fellow whose paintwork gets scraped and who leaps out of his car, fuming. Wife-batterers (as I write, twenty-two women have been killed so far this year) would have at their disposal not only their bare hands, petrol, knives and baseball bats with which to vent their fury on their victims, they would also be free to nip into a gunsmith's whenever they fancied and purchase a Barrett M90 with a telescopic lens as a way of getting round a restraining order. Gang members, neo-Nazis, and right-wing football hooligans would all have more than a dozen weapons each—accumulated patiently, month by month—not to mention the constant temptation to make use of them. Gunsmiths and the National Gun Association would agree with the views of the man who sold weapons to the Blacksburg nutter, namely, that if guns had been allowed on campus, there would have been far fewer deaths, because someone would have shot the psychopath halfway through his slaughter. Can you imagine Spaniards practising at home, like Jack Palance in *Shane*, to see who's quickest on the draw, just in case? This same sales clerk was even more clear-sighted when it came to defending the Second Amendment to the American Constitution, of only a couple of centuries ago, and which allows the population to bear arms: "Look, lady," he said to this newspaper's correspondent, "if it wasn't for my right to bear arms, I'd be speaking in a British accent and you'd be talking German." It requires a little thought to work out what he meant, but now I get it: the United States would still be a British colony and Spain would have been invaded by the Nazis, because, as everyone knows, it was freelance militiamen wearing Daniel Boone hats who defeated Hitler; Churchill and Stalin had nothing to do with it.

It's also a good idea to imagine people we know—whether in person or from the TV or radio—carrying a Ruger GP-100 or a Glock 17. We've all been infuriated by someone, even over dinner, and so from now on, I'm going to thank EU heaven that some of the people I've run into weren't armed. You have only to imagine certain irascible right-wingers being allowed to carry revolvers or, indeed, Aznar, Sarkozy or the infernal Kaczyński twins, to name but four, or should that be three, mean-looking dudes. Brussels forfend.

(2007)

No Narrative Shame*

Essentially the man is a bore, to judge by the videos in which he appears accompanied by other people, whether at summit meetings with fellow political leaders or at more frivolous social events. He behaves exactly the same in both situations, except that in the former he always pretends to be the host (even, say, in Canada) and in the latter he probably *is* the host, at least when the event takes place in Italy, but even when he's merely a guest, he has to dominate. Whenever he gets together with other heads of state, it's obvious that, deep down, he feels like an intruder, and it's precisely his jaunty, carefree manner—as I said, just as if he were the host or the guide wherever he happens to be—that betrays his deep-seated insecurity; it's as if he feared that at any moment a steward might come up to him and whisper discreetly in his ear that there has been a terrible mistake and he must leave the room, the office, the lunch, the summit, the ball. His unwavering contentment and self-confidence are excessive, like a phrase underlined in red. They may appear to be spontaneous, almost involuntary, but they're not: he has to make a constant effort (diluted only by habit) and, of course, he is always playing a part. His crazed (because permanent) smile, his jokes, his clowning, the way he embraces people and slaps them on the back,

* This text on Silvio Berlusconi was supplementary material arising from Marías's trilogy, *Your Face Tomorrow*.

his forwardness, his hyperactivity—as trivial as it is superfluous—are all pure acts of will. It's as if, at every moment, he were saying (to his political colleagues, to the cameras, to the photographers, to the viewers and above all to himself): "See how at ease I am, how well I handle myself, how I intrigue, how easily I fit into this world of global decision-making." The man himself doesn't quite believe it, in fact he doesn't believe it at all, which is why he has to make it absolutely clear that he is completely in his element.

He thinks that his friendliness (which is how he interprets it) brings him enormous benefits: in his own eyes he is captivating, irresistible, persuasive; he does not dare, however, to think of himself as sexually seductive. He uses friendliness, or so he thinks, as a means of acquiring things and of convincing other people of still more things, even people more powerful than him. And were his powerful colleagues not, in the main, rather dim (they give off very little light, managing to generate at most a faint penumbra), they would realize that this professional warmth is only Berlusconi's way of asking permission, of asking forgiveness, of craning his neck to ensure that no one obscures his face in the photo. I understand that for a while in his youth he was a crooner, or *cantante confidenziale* (as they say in Italian), who entertained the rich on cruises, or some such thing. As we know, such artistes, however famous they might be (and he was not), are, in the minds of the rich, much closer to the servant class than they are to the guests, and if my information is correct, he found it a useful training in how to break away and distance himself from the stewards and the waiters (when he's seen with them now, he may seem the soul of affability, but, deep down, he loathes them and tries to keep them at arm's length, for fear of contamination) and to mix instead with the more foolish and more gullible tycoons, those most susceptible to flattery. He has no qualms when it comes to flattery, sycophancy, or even obsequiousness. You might say that he has much in common with the old-style caretakers or porters who used to abound in Franco's Spain and who have still not entirely vanished: the kind who kowtow to the owners and to the wealthier tenants, but treat delivery men and servants like dirt.

This mentality is always a front for resentment. If such a person also has a terrible fear of appearing ridiculous, then the individual in question can prove dangerous, as could this man behind his façade of jokey cordiality and, one might almost say, "kindliness," if kindness—even in caricatured form—were not completely absent from his nature. The fact that he is occasionally moved or touched is irrelevant; such emotions are within the reach of any simpleton, and are not necessarily a sign of either kindness or compassion. It's incomprehensible really that anyone, far less an entire country, could have been taken in by him; it's incomprehensible that he should have been elected with an absolute majority, but then the same thing has happened many times before and in many countries. Mysteries. Or is it simply that people don't notice, don't pay attention, but look and listen only distractedly, the consequence perhaps of a televisual way of looking and listening? This man is unscrupulous, but in the most real and radical sense of the word: he isn't like those many other people who know that scruples exist, but choose not to bother with them; he doesn't know that they exist and so never thinks of them, not even as something to be dismissed as useless, stupid, costly or annoying. He has never rejected them for the simple reason that they are beyond his imagination and have never been a part of his thinking, let alone his values. So alien are they to him that when he notices them in someone else, he takes them as a sign of weakness and judges that person to be feeble or docile and therefore capable of being pushed around.

Most of us are defenceless against such people, because we are ill-equipped to deal with anyone as tiresome and insistent (a bore who cannot be still for a moment, the kind of man to whom one often says "Yes" purely in order to get rid of him, to interrupt his chatter and shut him up), someone apparently so agreeable and even affectionate, and yet who, at the same time, never abides by any rules or regulations. He has no rules to break, no principles to betray. He will never experience the feeling that he has gone too far or exceeded his authority or transgressed, although he might pretend to harbour such feelings, because he has noticed them in other people and learned how to copy them. However, the most difficult thing is this: almost no one is qualified to deal with a man who never feels any kind of shame, either personal, public, political or aesthetic. Nor any kind of narrative shame. He simply doesn't know the meaning of the term.

(2006)

All in Our Imagination

The dead are everywhere. Some have gravestones on which their names are engraved, others have nothing. Many are buried in cemeteries and churches, many beneath tarmac and in ditches and in fields, or wherever they happened to fall. There is probably no city or inhabited landscape that does not harbour human remains in its depths. Unaware of their presence, we trample them daily and lose no sleep over them. During all wars, communal graves are dug and bodies buried in great haste, just as they are during times of plague and major disasters. The seas, rivers and lakes also all contain corpses, for not every corpse floats to the surface. And now that cremation has become fashionable in our societies, the ashes of those who were once men and women are scattered who knows where. If we really believed that the dead did turn in their graves, every step we took would be sure to disturb someone.

Religions, which believe that the soul alone persists, are very contradictory in their custom of venerating the remains of the dead. Churches in Spain are full of the supposed relics of saints—a tibia, a femur, a skull, an arm untouched by corruption, a complete shrunken mummy—before which, over the centuries, the faithful have prostrated themselves, not knowing, as people are only now discovering, that most of those sacred remains in fact belonged to animals or, at best, to private individuals who lived in a very different age from that known by each martyr or saint. A religion like Catholicism, which believes in the resurrection of the flesh in some unearthly place, should care little about what happens to the bodies they so despise. Nonbelievers—of that religion or any other—should care even less. When someone dies, he ceases to exist except in memory; he is no longer there nor can he hear us, and only the habit of speaking to him and wondering what he would think or feel about this or that—a habit that may persist for a long time or, indeed, never cease—justifies our visiting the place where he was laid and addressing him through the headstone, as many characters in John Ford films do with great feeling. But why bother, why go to a cemetery or visit a grave when we can "speak" to the memory of the dead person in our own home or hear them answer us in dreams from which we wake feeling slightly troubled, half-sad and half-contented?

Attributing to someone's remains the desire to be in one place or another or to lie beside their loved ones can only be explained as superstition or as a "literary reflex" or as a form of religiosity even in those who claim to have no religious beliefs, but clearly do: it implies a belief that there is something beyond death and, even more disturbing, something that is contained inside the corpse. We all fantasize about such things, even when it comes to inanimate objects. A few years ago, I saw in the side window of an old shop two polychrome wooden figures. I took a fancy to one of them and went in to buy it. It was a kind of Hindu aide-de-camp dressed in a really lovely uniform. I took it home, but spent the whole day thinking about how I had separated him from the far more conventional and rather uninteresting Scottish piper who had kept him company in that narrow shop window for who knows how many years. And while I was engaged in thinking this nonsense, it occurred to me, too, that perhaps this was precisely what they both wanted, to be free of each other, because they were such an ill-matched couple. However, the fear that they might feel lonely got the better of me, and the following morning, I went back to the shop and bought the piper, even though I didn't want him at all.

The same puerile idea, if you'll forgive the comparison, lies behind the current obsession in Spain for recovering bones, only the bones of those who died in the Civil War, mind, not those of any other, even though Spain has had its fair share of wars. It's a perfectly respectable puerile idea and one that I understand—how could I not, when I've just confessed to one even more puerile—but if we start personifying those who are no longer persons and attributing desires to skeletons and remains, then one can just as easily imagine that perhaps those same remains have no desire to be disturbed or disinterred or moved, nor to be separated from the other unfortunates who died with them seventy or more years ago. According to these imaginings of ours—because they are ours and not theirs—how can anyone be sure that what remains of the person who was García Lorca wouldn't prefer to stay alongside those of the teacher and the *banderilleros* who accompanied him in his final hours and who, perhaps, cheered him and gave him courage? I don't know. An uncle of mine was murdered by militiamen in Madrid during the Civil War when he was only seventeen or eighteen. A victim of the losing side, his body has never been found and it's not known where he was buried. As far as I'm aware, neither my mother nor her other siblings went to any great pains to find him, and it wasn't the fact of not knowing where his body lay that caused them such grief and sorrow, but knowing that he had died in the flower of his youth and without a trial and for no reason. I've never spoken to them about it, but they might think it best not to move him or separate him from the young female friend and fellow student who was walking down the street with him when they were arrested and who met the same fate. They died together, comforting each other; may their bones, wherever they may be, continue to lie together.

(2008)

The Weekly Return to Childhood

The Cuban writer Guillermo Cabrera Infante loathes football. This could perhaps be explained by Cuba having little tradition of playing the sport, but Cabrera Infante's more than twenty-five years of living in England rather gives the lie to that. I remember his furious response to the tragedy at the Heysel Stadium. For once taking a different standpoint to Nabokov, who was a goalkeeper during his time at Cambridge University and always enjoyed watching matches on TV, Cabrera Infante did not blame the Liverpool fans, but the sport itself: "That dreadful game," he said, "provokes violence because it is itself violent: it's played with the feet, and there are few more violent actions than kicking someone." On the other hand, football has not prospered in the United States because it's considered too slow and dull, a lady's game. Indeed, when I taught for a few months at the all-female Wellesley College, the preferred sport was, to my great surprise, that of Di Stéfano. Of course, that could have been the influence of Nabokov, who passed through there in the 1950s and perhaps started the tradition.

There is no more agonizing sport when the game itself proves agonizing. More than that, in my own particular case, I have to say that it is one of the few things that elicits exactly the same response from me now as it did when I was ten years old and still a mere savage; it's a genuine weekly return to childhood. I had a real shock about a month ago: having no set-top box on my television, I had to follow the final match of the Spanish league on the radio, as I used to do in the post–Civil War years and even beyond. Perhaps that was what drew me back so powerfully to the wildest days of my childhood, but the fact is that when the match was over, my Barcelona-supporting publisher phoned me up with the Barça anthem playing in the background, all ready to make the kind of playful jokes we exchange by the hundred every month. And I told him in deadly seriousness that not only would I never allow him to publish any more of my books, I also doubted I would ever set foot in Barcelona again (and Barcelona is a city I love and where I have lived), nor, of course, would I ever set foot in Tenerife.* Out came the hooligan that all football fans carry within us.

Luckily, I got over it after a few hours—but that's how long it took—because there is a curse on football that is also the salvation of players, trainers and fans left downcast by a defeat. It is a game in which it is not enough just to win, you have to win every time, every season, every tournament, every game. A writer, an architect or a musician can rest a little after having written a great novel, designed a marvellous building or made an unforgettable record. They can choose to do nothing for a time or at least do something less important. Among the first group, which is the one I am most familiar with, some have been deemed to be good right up until their death, thanks to one estimable work written fifty years before. In football, on the other hand, there is no resting, no relaxing, because having an amazing track record or having won the title the previous year

---

* In the 1991–2 league season, Real Madrid lost the Spanish league to their arch-rivals, FC Barcelona, on a dramatic final day when they were defeated 3–2 by CD Tenerife.

counts for little. It is never over; footballers are required (and the players require this of themselves too) to win the next match as well, as if they were always starting from zero or nil, as they do at the beginning of every game. Unlike other activities in life, in sport (but especially in football), you don't accumulate or hoard anything, despite the rooms full of trophies and the ever more important statistics. Having been the best yesterday doesn't count today, let alone tomorrow. Past joy is as nothing compared to present anxiety, you cannot warm yourself on pleasant memories or on the satisfaction of past achievements, nor, of course, on the gratitude of the fans for the joy you brought them two weeks ago. On the other hand, sadness and indignation are equally short-lived, since this can, from one day to the next, be replaced by euphoria and sainthood. Perhaps that is why football is the sport, as Cabrera used to say, that provokes most violence, not because of all that kicking, but because of the anxiety it arouses. One invaluable aspect, however—which tends not to occur elsewhere in life—is that it also provokes forgetting, which is tantamount to saying that it never provokes rancour, something you learn only when you reach adulthood.

(1992)

Why Almost No One
Can Be Trusted

When you think about it or look back or remember, you will probably find that you know hardly anyone who does not claim to place some rather impersonal and abstract ideal or entity above his or her relationships with other people. There is a particular form of words that is repeated spontaneously in all kinds of situations, and not only is it accepted, it generally gives rise to expressions of praise and admiration. The person saying it is usually greeted with applause and seen as an example of commitment, self-abnegation, altruism and even loyalty. It's just as likely to be heard, with variations naturally, in the mouths of footballers, politicians and guerrillas, and, of course, in the mouths of nationalists and clerics of any religion, whose raison d'être it is. I, on the other hand, find it a disquieting, not to say aberrant thing to say, and it immediately makes me distrust the person using it in any one of its infinite varieties. The form of words in question always claims that something, usually something that does not exist— or is, at most, ungraspable, intangible, amorphous or invisible—is "above" everything else and, naturally, above other people: God or the Church, Spain, Catalonia or Euskal Herria, the company, the party, ideology, the State, the revolution, communism, fascism, the capitalist system, justice, the law, the language, this or that institution, this school, this newspaper, this bank, the Crown, the Republic, the

Army, a name, this or that TV channel, a particular brand, Barcelona football club or Real Madrid, my family, my principles, my country. Anything, from the grandiose to the trivial, can be deemed to be "above" mere people, and those who espouse that belief have no qualms about sacrificing or betraying individuals in the name of what they consider to be "sacred" or "the cause," whether it be an ideal, a chimera or, more likely, a mere disembodied fantasy.

There is almost no difference between what Islamist suicide bombers shout at the moment prior to death ("God is great," I think it is) and the first of Christianity's Ten Commandments ("Thou shalt have no other gods before me," at least it was when I studied it). The rest are variants or copies of that absolutist affirmation, applied to whatever happens to tickle the fancy of the idiot of the moment, from "Everything for the Fatherland," which may or may not still be found inscribed above the doors of Spanish army barracks, to the "Bolivarian Socialist Revolution," or whatever it is that Hugo Chávez calls his totalitarian project in Venezuela, and every other possible variation in between: "the ancestral Basque people," "Rule Britannia," "*Deutschland über alles*," "the great Russian fatherland," or the Treasury Department, *The Times*, *Le Monde*, Manchester United, Juventus, the Monarchy, the Constitution, the BBC, the Papacy, the Cultural Revolution, and not forgetting, of course, "the sovereign people," and the name of just about any multinational or local company.

The phrase in question is often topped off by another similar, still more explicit one: "People pass, institutions remain," as if the latter, from the Church to Athletic Bilbao, were not the work and invention of people, and in fact existed to serve them rather than the other way round. The truth is that for far too many centuries, we have been encouraged to believe that we are all at the service of something intangible whose perpetuity takes precedence over us. It is not, then, so very odd that these categorical, vacuous statements should enjoy such a magnificent reputation, nor that those who cease to subscribe to them should be treated as if they had the plague. Do you mean that you're not prepared to sacrifice everything for the company? A soldier who is not prepared to die for his country whatever the circumstances? A revolutionary unwilling to betray his neighbours? One of the faithful who has doubts about blowing himself up in order to kill three infidels? A believer who chooses to renounce his faith rather than embrace martyrdom? A footballer who prefers to accept a juicy financial package rather than stay with the club that nurtured him? There you have examples of an egotist, a coward, a turncoat, a traitor, an apostate and a money-grubber. Anyone who doesn't place something above himself, above other people and above their feelings is greeted with insults and scorn.

And yet . . . I feel much safer and more comfortable in the company of those who lack that "superior" loyalty, who never place an abstraction above their concern for those close to them, who will turn against me only because of something I have done, rather than because of some dogma or belief or ideal. More than that, they are the *only* people I trust, whereas I could never trust a religious leader or a politician or a soldier or a nationalist, or indeed a believer or a militant or an official patriot, because I know that any one of them would be prepared to betray me or sacrifice me. If it came to it, they would be the vassals and unconditional supporters of what they have placed "above" all else even if they disapprove of the behaviour of those who embody that ideal. So widespread is this feeling that I find there is almost no one I can trust. And, viewed through that prism, you, too, will see—if you think about it or look back or remember— how very few people can be trusted.

(2009)

In Praise of the Egotist

There are many types of egotist, and literature abounds in them, from the misanthropic Pío Baroja to the ecumenical Thomas Mann, as well as almost every poet who has ever lived, with Juan Ramón Jiménez and Rainer Maria Rilke at their head, poets who sacrificed everything (mainly their fellow men and women) to compose a few lines of poetry in silence and solitude. There is no shortage of fictional egotists either, from the mean Dickensian Scrooge of *A Christmas Carol* to the cruel and suffering Adolphe, protagonist of Benjamin Constant's novel, whose direct heir is Marcel, the narrator of *In Search of Lost Time*, the most pitiless observer of humanity in all of twentieth-century literature.

And that is perhaps the great virtue and advantage of the egotist: his or her capacity to observe without experiencing any obligation to feel pity. It is said of generous, altruistic people that they are capable of putting themselves in someone else's shoes and of understanding their needs, but this can inevitably give rise to a high degree of confusion: the altruist—who is, deep down, a stickler for the rules—ends up believing that everyone's desires and needs are the same, and thus performs a kind of levelling process, the effect of which is to make those individuals replace their possible previous desires with others that the altruist considers universal. Now that is precisely what no one wants, since our most authentic desires are unique and untransferable and, often, unconfessable. The egotist, on the other hand, tends to know himself through and through and is never likely to confuse himself with someone else, still less usurp another's personality. And because he is not equipped to place himself in that other person's shoes, he will never cease to see other people as individuals with their own interests and desires, which he deems to be as worthy of respect as his own. The egotist will be able to discriminate, discern and see more clearly because he doesn't compare or involve himself with others. The egotist weighs his words, his actions and his power, and in doing so, even though his objective is always his own best interests, and although one might say that, as a whole, he lacks scruples, the advantage is that he will behave with urbanity, civility and tact, and can at least claim to be free of the two gravest and most widespread sins of our age: proselytism and messianism. The egotist is one of the few people not trying to convert or save anyone, and is, therefore, one of the few capable of seeing the truth.

(1990)

All Too Few

A few of my female friends are reaching an age when their sons or daughters are beginning to leave home; and since, sometimes, I'm so obtuse that I can only think about and fix on what is there before me—a form of obtuseness, let it be said in my defence, that I believe I share with most of my fellow men and women—I cannot help but reflect on the silent, private sadness "that dare not speak its name" with which these mothers confront the emptying of their homes. It's not surprising they keep quiet about it and conceal it. My friends are intelligent and generous women. They know that it's good for their offspring to leave home, whether to get married or something similar, out of a desire for adventure or independence or out of mere impatience to incorporate themselves fully into the world. They know, too, that they're not losing their children, they will simply cease to live with them and, often, cease taking care of them in the more prosaic and everyday ways: they will no longer have to cook for them or take them to the doctor or turn on the washing machine to do their laundry, or put up with their deafening music or their occasional bad manners. They know that their children must now learn things for themselves, take on responsibilities and gain experience; and that if they do linger in the paternal or maternal home (as happens with ever greater frequency, because of the increasingly high cost of housing and the precarious nature of employment), they, the mothers, would be the first to worry and to encourage and help them find their own territory. So they know that they have no objective reasons to complain or feel sad. And, of course, it cannot escape them that they did exactly the same when they were young, and did so without a twinge of bad conscience.

However, another reason why their discretion doesn't surprise me is that mothers are often the easy target of affectionate derision. Remarks such as "Oh, you know what mothers are like" or "You sound just like my mother" are commonplace, and while they may be affectionate, they're also slightly scornful, in particular comments along the lines of "Mothers are such a drag." In films, of course, mothers tend to be shown weeping at the weddings of their "little ones," out of an excess of sentimentality and a lack of self-control, and are deemed more deserving of gentle mockery than compassion and understanding. When I look at my female friends now, I think their reasons for weeping are far more respectable than mere superficial and rather exhibitionist emotion, because, like it or not, a long period of their existence is coming to a close, and their life will never be the same. I have so much respect for the pain caused when something ends that I can even understand those who regret—although they will rarely confess or admit to it—the death of a long-time enemy or the resolution of an unsatisfactory situation. Because one can also miss struggle, effort, resistance, habit. Conrad said that the only thing that saved sailors from despair when they went to sea, not to return for a long time, was "soothing routine," the routine that made them get up each morning during the first few days of the voyage. That's why it's so hard to lose routines, however unsatisfactory.

I can think of only one film that views such abandoned mothers with sympathy and sensitivity, even though the mother in question is actually the maiden aunt who brought Captain Gregg up after he was orphaned as a child. That captain is the protagonist of one of my all-time favourites, *The Ghost and Mrs. Muir* by Joseph Mankiewicz. The captain set sail for the first time at sixteen. When Lucy Muir asks what his aunt did when he ran away to sea, the ghost replies: "Oh, probably thanked heaven there was no one around to fill her house with mongrel puppies and track mud on her carpets." Lucy Muir remains thoughtful, and the captain asks her what she's thinking. "I'm thinking how lonely she must have felt," Lucy says, "with her clean carpets." It's just a detail, but it's the only example I can recall of a fictional character putting herself in the modest place of those mothers.

And of course all this leads me to remember my own mother when I left home at twenty-three to go and live in another city with a married woman separated from her husband. Naturally, I didn't give a moment's thought then to the sadness I see now in my female friends whose children are going away. Life is really very badly organized: when we're young, we're aware of so little, certainly not of our parents, whom we tend to see as suffocating, intrusive beings, who get in our way and stop us doing what we want to do, almost as a burden. Only much later, once we're over thirty (if we're lucky) can we start to see them as people who were, have been and are something more than just our parents. Then comes curiosity, and even the desire to make it up to them, to listen to them properly, to look at them clearly, to pay them more attention, to ponder their feelings and anxieties not just about us, because we were not always the centre of their lives, even though in our youthful vanity it seemed to us that we were. And sometimes this comes too late. I only returned to my mother's house to watch her die, three years later. And now when I see the private sadness of my friends whose children are leaving aged twenty-five or thirty (although, as mothers, my friends still keep alive the memory of all the other years, from zero on), I realize that my mother only had me near her for twenty-three, and that those twenty-three years must have seemed to her all too few.

(2006)

DUSTY SPECTACLE

Damned Artists!

Fortunately, very few children want to be artists or writers when they grow up. *That* is something which—with the odd repellent exception—one simply ends up becoming or turns out to be. Even though I enjoyed reading as a child, I think the last thing I would have said in response to the classic question was "a novelist." A pirate, a footballer, an archaeologist (yes, long before Indiana Jones), a bandit, a lion-tamer, even perhaps, in an attack of folly, a doctor . . . I've no idea what children nowadays would like to be when they grow up, but I'm sure they don't aspire to devoting their lives to literature, painting or "serious" music. Just as well, because, as I did fifty years ago, they would find it hard to identify with artists as they're represented in films and, indeed, books, and they certainly wouldn't want to emulate them. The most worrying thing for those of us who *have* turned out to be novelists or poets or sculptors or painters or musicians is that not even as adults have we seen much reason to admire our predecessors as people. We might feel great admiration for their work, but we rarely take to them when their lives are recounted in books or depicted on screen. I don't know if it's just that our profession has been particularly unfortunate in that respect or if we really are unbearable.

The truth is that artists are usually seen as megalomaniacs and, very often, as loudmouths, who suffer greatly and cut off their ear or *pretend* to be suffering and drag themselves histrionically through the mud; who take themselves very seriously and are, by and large, vain, ambitious and rather on the stingy side; who, with unbelievable frequency, slide into some form of addiction (alcohol, drugs, gambling) which leads them to inflict the most bizarre and harmful behaviour on their loved ones; who find it equally difficult to cope with either success or failure and require unhealthily large doses of attention; who determinedly get themselves into inadvisable situations and set off along gratuitously dangerous, self-destructive paths; who strive at all times to be brilliant and deep, which is tiring for them and tiresome in the extreme for those around them, as well as for the reader or viewer; they also take pride in being enigmatic, which is a dreadful bore; plus they're obsessed with their work, which is all that really exists for them. So I've seen Scott Fitzgerald getting drunk as a lord while wearing Gregory Peck's face; Michelangelo throwing one almighty tantrum wearing Charlton Heston's face; Picasso endlessly misbehaving and wearing, I believe, Jeremy Irons's face; Beethoven being proud and grandiloquent wearing Ed Harris's face; and Mozart playing the fool wearing the face of the now forgotten Tom Hulce; not to mention the seamier side of Van Gogh, Rimbaud, Bob Dylan, Truman Capote, Frida Kahlo and her husband (well, with a couple like that, what can you expect?), and hundreds more. Speaking from a purely personal point of view, the experience has served to make me try to be as unlike them as possible in my own life, even at the cost of abjuring characteristics that many people—not children, but adolescents and adultescents—associate with talent and genius: there are still those who believe that drinking to excess, pumping themselves full of drugs or driving erratically will make them more like Faulkner, Lowry or the inevitable Kerouac, Burroughs and Bukowski.

This was why, in part, I was interested to watch the German TV series *The Mann Family*, made in 2001 and newly issued on DVD. Thomas Mann was not noted for his unusual or anomalous behaviour. He was forced into exile during the Nazi regime, but apart from that, suffered few setbacks or hardships and led a reasonably respectable life. The life of his eldest son, Klaus, a not inconsiderable writer himself, was rather more shocking and ended in suicide. There was, then, nothing in Thomas Mann as a character that might lend itself to the excesses and exhibitionism that beset almost every artist depicted on screen or in literature. "Perhaps I will at last find an artist whom I like," I thought, "someone I wouldn't have minded knowing." No such luck. Thomas Mann appears neither irascible nor hysterical, he doesn't live in a permanent torment of doubt or poised on the edge of the "abyss of creation." He seems more like a notary or a factory-owner, and his one caprice—for a father of a large family—is a kind of abstract homosexuality that manifests itself only in half-furtive glances at handsome young men. Not a very attractive character, but sober enough. And yet his seems more an example to flee than to follow: a kind of pumice stone, rough and brittle, who doesn't even get upset over his own son Klaus's first suicide attempt. A smug, solemn individual, who receives the news that he has won the Nobel Prize with unseemly nonchalance, as if it were only to be expected or were simply his due. He's someone keenly aware of his own celebrity and appears to share his wife's estimate of him when she interviews a candidate for the post of secretary to the writer, warning her: "We will require absolute confidentiality on your part. After all, he *is* Thomas Mann!" To judge by this worthwhile and interesting series, the author of *The Magic Mountain* must have got up in the mornings, looked at himself in the mirror and exclaimed reverently: "Gosh, I'm Thomas Mann!" I don't know if we'll ever be able to see a film about an artist or read a book about his or her life without it making us wonder if our admiration for the work of such a creature hasn't been a big mistake.

(2008)

Dusty Spectacle

In a world of ever more but ever less enduring books, the survival of the antiquarian bookshops that sell second-hand books—that is, used books, previously owned books, or whatever you choose to call them—is, in itself, a spectacle worthy of note. True, their quality varies from country to country, and although some attractive ones are to be found in Spain, where they warrant a whole block of stalls at the two annual book fairs held in Recoletos in Madrid, their true domain lies in England. Not only do such shops never close down, they occasionally move to better or larger premises. The main reason for this, I believe, is not sociological, it is not because the English read more voraciously than other Europeans, but physical, because in England, books have usually been published first in hardback, which is why the books do not perish, but are passed endlessly from hand to hand without suffering any harm. One should perhaps add another somewhat idiosyncratic reason: England has far more cranks and eccentrics than any other country, and its inhabitants are of a naturally investigative bent.

In one way, this literary underworld represents the world in reverse, or perhaps a brave negation of the present, where the kind of books you see on display everywhere in ordinary book-shops, standing stacked in vertiginous piles alongside gigantic posters displaying the author's generally ill-tempered face, the books that, week after week, will top the best-seller lists and whose titles will be on everyone's lips for, at most, a couple of months, are precisely the ones that will never find a place in the literary under-world and will always be rejected by the second-hand bookseller when included in a batch of books for sale. In his world, an initial print run of tens of thousands is a positive blot, because such a book will be of little value. On the other hand, a limited edition, never to be repeated, means that, a few years after its birth, the book in question will have appreciated, not depreciated in value, as will have happened with the best seller. Obviously, in order to reach that thrilling, belated and all too often posthumous kingdom, it is not enough for a book to be rare or for there to be only a few copies available; its creator also has to become what is known as a "cult author," or (which comes to the same thing) someone with a small but growing band of fanatical admirers who want to own every line he or she ever wrote and are prepared to pay large sums of money for a signed or dedicated copy.

Deep down, all readers, however unconsciously, share that same fetishistic urge. Who wouldn't want to own a volume signed by Baudelaire or Dickens, Wilde or Cervantes, Voltaire or Faulkner? Each signed or dedicated copy is unique, quite different from all the other books in the same print run, which is why such copies sell for high prices and why real collectors do battle for them against mere accumulators of wealth (namely, American universities). What makes those signatures priceless—signatures that the authors doubt-less dashed off distractedly or even reluctantly—is the fact that the writers are dead, which means that a new signature is now unobtain-able. And that is only the first necrophiliac element in this increasingly strange business. The people who inhabit this under-world of old books (and, less blatantly, the world of books in general, not to mention the world of art) are always waiting, and waiting mostly for death. First, they wait for the titles to go out of print and become unavailable anywhere; then they wait to see which writers evolve, over time, into great figures, objects of worship or sad nobodies; then they wait for the deaths of the generations of buyers whose children, it is assumed, will not like the same writers as their parents and will thus put back into circulation books with which their progenitors would never willingly have parted; and, finally, they wait for the deaths of the authors themselves.

There is, of course, no impatience, no ill feeling in this waiting. Second-hand booksellers tend to be very respectful of writers; indeed, their need to make money will find them torn between a secret longing for an author's early demise (when first editions and signed copies will rise in value) and a genuine desire for their longevity, thus ensuring an increase (although not too great an increase) in the number of titles, editions and possibly dedicated copies—all food and drink to the bookseller. The latter will not be deceived by those wily authors who, in order to make money in that underworld while still alive and kicking, will sign anything that comes their way and sell off whatever manuscripts, drafts, letters, postcards and scraps of paper cross their desk on a daily basis. I remember an employee of Bertram Rota in London explaining to me why books signed by the obscure author John Gawsworth were of such little value: "Apart from the fact that he is such an obscure figure," he told me, "he was so poor at the end of his life that he would slap his signature on almost anything in an attempt to up the price of his books and his library." In that sense, booksellers are very particular: a book dedicated by Virginia Woolf to some unknown is not as valuable as a book dedicated to one of her colleagues, E. M. Forster, for example. The basic idea is that the book in question will have passed through *two* pairs of literary or famous hands, thus doubling its value. The underworld's ideal object would be a book that various writers had passed from one to another and in which each left his or her signature. If such a thing existed, however, one would inevitably suspect that the now priceless book had perhaps been loathed by all of them, which is why they kept giving it away, passing it swiftly on to someone else.

I should say that, even though I know this underworld well, I, too, like to own signed copies of books by my contemporaries (although not all of them). A lot of people despise the signing sessions held at book fairs and in large shops because they seem not only too easy, but also free and available to anyone. I, however, take them very seriously, knowing that, while most of the dedications will be destroyed either by time or by the buyer's heirs, in a hundred years or so, someone will feel as excited to come across a signed copy of a book by Juan Benet or Eduardo Mendoza as we would if we owned a book signed by Valle-Inclán or Larra.

One of the British booksellers who has, for some years now, been supplying me with interesting oddities is Ben Bass, although I have never actually met him, since his house-cum-bookshop is located in some out-of-the-way place in the countryside, near the River Avon. He has, apparently, deliberately chosen to have very few customers: he will not sell books to just anyone, but only to people who have been "recommended" by a previous client or who, from the start, have come to him with "interesting requests." We have exchanged numerous letters and spoken on the phone. His voice seems out of keeping with such punctiliousness, being hoarse and rather uneducated, more suited to a sailor than to a scholar, and there's no bargaining with him either. If he asks for twenty pounds and I suggest paying eighteen, he'll immediately increase the price to twenty-five, so confident is he of his sales and his clientele. Choosing one's customers, unthinkable in any new business, is quite a frequent practice among second-hand booksellers. And one of the most painful things I have ever seen is the terrible doubt that gripped a certain lady bookseller who was also a collector—a combination doomed to tragedy. On the one hand, she wanted to sell as many books as possible, since that was how she made her living, but, on the other hand, she hoped, quite unreasonably, that no one would come into her shop or express an interest in any of her treasures, because she had such a choice selection of books that it pained her to let any of them go and thus ruin the whole collection. Her name was Veronica Watts, and she bore a striking resemblance to the actress Anne Bancroft and the writer Susan Sontag. She collected everything written by or about one of history's greatest eccentrics, William Beckford, and would interrogate her customers about his life and works.

Other second-hand booksellers treat their business as, well, a business. They are cold and imperturbable and probably never read anything. The only things they understand are paper, ink, editions, dates, print runs, covers, dedications and signatures, and they are experts in their field. They care about everything but the contents of a book. I visited such a bookseller once to sell him a couple of gems I had picked up for a song and which I imagined were quite valuable. The bookseller eyed the books sceptically at first. "Hmm," he said, "I know these, I've seen similar editions before" (which are the most discouraging words a would-be seller can hear). "I'll buy them though," he added, "because I've never seen this dust jacket with this particular advert on it. It's the first time Beckett's name appears in print; the other one is intriguing too because it still has the left flap, which most people cut off and keep whenever they manage to buy a copy." On that left flap was the photograph taken of Isak

Dinesen disguised as a man when her novel *The Angelic Avengers* was first published under the male pseudonym of Pierre Andrézel. Needless to say, as soon as I left the shop, clutching my precious pound notes, I immediately regretted not having cut off that unusual left flap and, worse, having sold a wonderful, historic dust jacket that I will never ever find again.

(1990)

My Favourite Book

Asking a writer to choose his favourite book is tempting him either to lie or to boast, since, if he's really honest (not that there's any reason why he should be, either then or on any other occasion), he would be sure to say that his favourite book is one that he himself has written. It isn't the case, as the late, boastful Juan Rulfo said about his novel *Pedro Páramo*, that all writers write the book they would like to read, because otherwise there would be nothing worth reading, but it is true that an author's own books are the ones he will have read most often and with most care, patience, interest, understanding and indulgence (sometimes as if his very life depended on it). They will also be the books—one presumes—that most satisfy him, and if they're not, then he should refrain from publishing them. Writing is, in short, the most perfect and passionate way of reading, which is doubtless why adolescents, who usually have more time on their hands, often take the trouble to write out a poem they really love: copying out is not only a way of appropriating a text, of adopting and endorsing it, it's also the best, most exact, most alert, most certain way of reading it. The Borges character Pierre Menard set out to write *Don Quixote* and, before he died, managed to complete two whole chapters and a fragment by his own means (that is, not by copying or transcribing it or even trying to live the same life Cervantes lived in order to find out if it was those experiences that had led him to write the book). His work, therefore, remained unfinished—a very painful and frustrating experience for any writer—even though, in his case, Menard could, had he so wished, have easily found out what the rest of his novel would have been like. Of course, being a writer rather than a mere reader, he did not.

I, however, am fortunate enough to be able to reply to the question without indulging in lies or even in excessive vainglory because I translated Laurence Sterne's *Tristram Shandy* (or *The Life and Opinions of Tristram Shandy, Gentleman* to give it its full title), and so, as well as reading it, I have also written it. It probably is and will be my best book, and I say "probably" thinking of other translations I've done (*The Mirror of the Sea* by Conrad or the works of Sir Thomas Browne) or others I might one day consider undertaking (Eliot's "Prufrock" or Faulkner's *The Wild Palms*).

Now, when I say that *Tristram Shandy* is my favourite book, I realize that this is precisely because I did translate it, because each and every one of its sentences, every word (even the blank and, indeed, the black pages it contains) not only passed before my attentive gaze, but through my painstaking intellect, my vigilant ear, my own tongue (by which I mean Spanish, not the moist thing in my mouth), and were finally reordered and set down on paper by my weary, hard-working fingers. Had I not translated *Tristram Shandy*, my favourite book might be *Don Quixote* or *Madame Bovary* or *Heart of Darkness* or *Adolphe* or the poetry of Baudelaire. However, I didn't spend almost two years of my life with any of those books; nor did I submerge myself in them as I did in *Tristram Shandy*, however carefully I may have read them (and I did have to read *Don Quixote* in order to teach it, which is another of the most perfect ways of reading a book, but not the most exciting); none of them obliged me to write or edit or compose over a thousand sheets of paper, each one typed and retyped numerous times; none demanded that I find or invent more than a thousand notes; none of them, lastly, took over my prose, put me inside the author's—the other's—skin, so that I thought like him, spoke like him, said what he said in the way that he said it. Consequently, I can announce the title of my favourite book without resorting to lies. And yet, even though the truth does not impel me (as it would most writers) to choose one of my own novels, such absolute sincerity does not entirely exempt me from a charge of boastfulness.

For I should, in all honesty, say that my favourite book is my *Tristram Shandy*, that is, *Tristram Shandy* in or according to my version, which is necessarily different from Sterne's (although it's also necessarily the same, which is one of the insoluble paradoxes of translation, of all translation, good or bad), just as the two chapters of *Don Quixote* that Pierre Menard managed to write must have been different from those by Cervantes even though they were exactly the same, word for word, and written in the same language. This doesn't mean that I consider my version of Sterne's novel to be superior to Sterne's original—no, I mean something much simpler and less competitive: in my version, in Sterne-according-to-Marías, I know the reasoning behind the choice of each line and each word, whereas I don't in Sterne-according-to-Sterne. And that is why I could still go on correcting my version, could keep working on it, improving it in accordance with my current criteria, aptitudes and understanding (the translation was, after all, published in 1978), something that I couldn't and wouldn't want to do with the English text, which, unlike the Spanish, does not in any way belong to me.

There's another circumstance to be added to all of this, one that apparently contradicts what I've just said and yet which is crucial to me in making my choice. The further beyond my grasp a book is, the greater my admiration. There are books I wouldn't want to write and wouldn't like to have written and which I nonetheless admire, precisely because, quite apart from not wanting to have written them, I feel I would have been incapable of doing so. Of all the books I've written or translated, and which I know, therefore, that in one sense or another I was capable of writing or translating, *Tristram Shandy* is the only book I would consider myself incapable of writing or translating now, even though I know that I *did* translate it. I mean if, say, just for the pleasure of reading a page or two, I open it at random and start to read (to re-read my own version), I find myself confronted by a task that now seems to me utterly impossible. I cannot conceive of how anyone could translate or have translated each and every page of this book into Spanish in an acceptable manner, and I can't explain how the person I was did just that. I don't believe the person I am now would be capable of the task. My favourite book, then, contains all the necessary qualities to be my favourite: it is, at once, the classic novel closest to *Don Quixote* and to the novel of my own age; thinking about it and occasionally dipping into it always bring me pleasure; and, finally, I admire it immensely because I see it as something beyond my grasp, even though I know that, as well as reading it (which, fortunately, I will always be able to do), there was a time when I re-wrote it.

(1989)

This Childish Task

Most of my bookshelves are guarded, protected and defended by small tin soldiers from various armies and eras; one shelf is even under the protection of a civilian population, not made of tin this time, but of hard, high-quality German plastic. The soldiers are arranged in ranks and are all of the same size or pretty much in proportion, both those on foot and those on horse- or camel-back (there are a lot of colonial troops), whereas the civilians are a chaotic mixture, belonging to very different social spheres (there are even wild animals and racehorses galloping past train passengers laden down with luggage and past dancing couples), and some look like giants beside the smaller ones, while the latter look like Lilliputians beside the former. I suppose this isn't entirely coincidental, although I tend to believe that it is. In civil society, everything is less orderly and more confused, discipline is minimal (if it isn't, it means we're living under a dictatorship, and having suffered under one of those for far too long I certainly don't want another one, not even on my bookshelves), and so, in a way, all kinds of absurdities, inconsistencies and monstrosities are acceptable. In real armies, as in novels, this is impossible or, at the very least, inadvisable.

I suppose that this liking of mine for diminutive worlds has two sides to it: one childish, one literary—although this perhaps amounts to the same thing. It clearly has its roots in part in my childhood.

Children have an extraordinary capacity for noticing the very tiny, but more than that, for penetrating and inhabiting and breathing fictional life into it. I don't know how it is nowadays, but boys' fantasies always used to be either military or athletic in tone and found expression in disguises, toy soldiers and, if you were lucky, a toy fort that was repeatedly besieged by Indians; girls, I imagine, concentrated on, became absorbed by or wrapped up in the sheer tininess of doll's houses (that was the norm, although there were always exceptions and reversals: bellicose girls and domesticated boys); for both, however, this was an initiation into fiction. By which I mean creative fiction, invented by them and full of all kinds of possibilities, a fiction in which they were obliged to invent the story, the adventure, the plot, however schematic or mimetic these might be; comics, films and books, on the other hand, represented fiction received or inherited, but which, in turn, served as models and stimuli for creation or re-creation. When you think about it, those games in which—by following certain rules or conventions, and trying always to keep within the bounds of plausibility—one decided the fates and vicissitudes of soldiers or dolls were probably a first decisive step towards writing fiction. Or, of course, filming it.

The fact that my bookshelves are still crowded with tin soldiers is due in part, I think, to my refusal entirely to lose sight of the very modest origins of the novels I write. Hanging on to them as an adult, keeping them there before me in serried ranks, prepared and on guard, is, in a way, a reminder of the childish nature of what has been my principal occupation over many days and many years now, a salutary puncturing of the importance of that task (there's nothing worse for a writer than to take himself too seriously and to believe that what he's doing is important or even significant), as well as an act of loyalty. I always keep in mind those lines by Robert Louis

Stevenson in which, when he compares himself to his ancestors, who were builders of lighthouses, he cannot help but feel the insignificance of his chosen trade, and he begs for a little understanding: "Say not of me that weakly I declined/The labours of my sires, and fled the sea,/The towers we founded and the lamps we lit,/To play at home with paper like a child."

I try not only to remind myself that this really is all I do—namely, devote myself "to this childish task," as Stevenson calls it in the same poem ("But rather say: *In the afternoon of time/A strenuous family dusted from its hands/The sand of granite, and beholding far/Along the sounding coast its pyramids/And tall memorials catch the dying sun,/Smiled well content, and to this childish task/Around the fire addressed its evening hours*")—I also like to have before me the probable origin of my chosen career, to have it there physically, corporeally, in that large army of silent, expectant, motionless figures who, nevertheless, like the characters in a novel when a novel is still in its very early stages of being written, seem as if they might start walking and talking and thus experiencing some possible story of which I was the sole witness and which, therefore, no one else can tell.

(2005)

For Me Alone to Read

A couple of weeks ago I wrote about how certain lines from books and films and certain pieces of music which we once thought wonderful can sometimes become so hackneyed that we can barely stand to hear them any more. This is the case, above all, with books, but something similar and even more mysterious happens with films and music. Every fan of these arts has experienced, at least in youth, the feeling of "appropriating" whatever he or she reads, sees and listens to. The sense that these works were made for you alone. That the author's voice or the director's images or the composer's notes were intended solely for us (that is, "for me"), and that we were the only people who knew them, or at least the ones who best or most truly understood them. Needless to say, you gradually come to realize that many other readers, viewers or listeners are familiar with these works and have perhaps felt the same, and then you cannot help but see these others as "usurpers" or "copycats." When devotees of a particular writer, director or composer find that the latter have grown too successful or have too many admirers, it's not unusual for them to desert them, if I can put it like that, or else join the ranks of the disaffected or even of their detractors. It's as if we thought: "Well, if all those other people like them, I'm off." This isn't simply an elitist position—although it is that too—or because it's impossible to belong to the "initiated few" when there are legions of initiates, it's that we feel somehow "dispossessed" ("This no longer belongs only to me") or that our favourites have become contaminated.

It's even worse when we discover that we share passions with people we don't like, or whom we detest or despise, or who strike us as arrant fools. Obviously this happens with the classics. Two years ago, we all had "our own" *Don Quixote* and probably each of us felt that most of the many others were spouting nonsense whenever they talked about the book, even though we all shared the same enthusiasm. We perhaps had a private belief that our reading was the "right" one and rather crazily continued to believe that Cervantes had written it almost exclusively for us. It's even harder to see people we consider to be utter idiots suddenly discovering one of our favourite authors and starting to quote from him and to comment on him, in short, to "appropriate" him, and in doing so they often almost ruin him for us. For example, if a columnist in the habit of pawing everything he touches, and usually spoiling it in the process, should suddenly be dazzled by G. K. Chesterton and proceed to write about him constantly, transforming him into some awful, over-pious fellow, we cannot help but feel that our jovial Chesterton has been "soiled" in some way or that, as far as we are concerned, he has been rendered useless. And if we hear someone for whom we have little respect declaring that his favourite films are the same as ours, let's say: *The Searchers, Two Rode Together* and *The Man Who Shot Liberty Valance*, we experience a feeling of profanation. They will, of course, feel exactly the same when they hear us praising Chesterton (although not, of course, for being pious) or John Ford's three crowning achievements. Obviously, none of us is right, and that's why I speak of feelings rather than judgements.

The extraordinary thing about literature (and perhaps to a lesser degree films and music, because in these other arts there is no voice telling and persuading and whispering, and it is the narrative voice that most captivates) is that once you know that nothing is yours alone and that you might share enthusiasms with those you most despise, the puerile feeling nevertheless prevails that no one has read such-and-such an author or such-and-such a work in the same way as you have. Our personal experience survives and, despite all our "disillusionments," we nevertheless go on believing that the writer was writing only for us. After the recent centenary celebrations for Hergé, the creator of Tintin, it has been impossible not to recognize, if we hadn't already, that Tintin and Haddock belong to the whole of humanity. And yet nothing can erase the excitement I felt as a child when I first read the comic books, just as nothing will erase the excitement felt by Arturo Pérez-Reverte, to mention just one Tintinophile, who even, in part, imitated him by choosing to follow a career as a reporter.* Both of us—and millions more—will continue to think: "Those stories were written for me alone to look at and read." That's the wonderful thing: even though men have been reading the *Iliad* for centuries and we are not discovering anything new when we cast our eyes over it, that act of reading is ours alone and the work in question is then as new as if Homer had just composed it. No one can take that away from us. I remember reading *Madame Bovary* while staying, alone and frightened, in a country house in Gerona, with dogs barking in the distance. For me that is the only

---

* Arturo Pérez-Reverte is a contemporary Spanish novelist and columnist who embarked on a career as a reporter and war reporter in the 1970s, before beginning to write in the 1980s. He is of Javier Marías's generation (they were both born in 1951) and they have become good friends over the years. Their friendship started by way of the dialogue they initiated through their weekly newspaper columns, which were published in the same supplement in the 1990s.

Madame Bovary that exists, however many learned studies and wise interpretations may have been written about it. It's fortunate really that we are not all granted the wish expressed by the Woody Allen character in *Annie Hall*, who, standing in line at a cinema, listening to some guy pontificating foolishly and pedantically about McLuhan, wishes that McLuhan himself would appear and say to the idiot behind him: "You know nothing of my work." Who knows, it might be us and not the others who Cervantes or Homer, Flaubert, John Ford or Chesterton decided to take down a peg or two.

(2007)

Hating The Leopard

There is no such thing as the indispensable book or author, and the world would be exactly the same if Kafka, Proust, Faulkner, Mann, Nabokov and Borges had never existed. It might not be quite the same if none of them had existed, but the nonexistence of just one of them would certainly not have affected the whole. That is why it is so tempting—an easy temptation if you like—to think that *the* representative twentieth-century novel must be the one that very nearly didn't exist, the one that nobody would have missed (Kafka, after all, did not leave just the one work, and as soon as it was known that there were others, as well as *Metamorphosis*, any reader was then at liberty to desire or even yearn to read them), the one novel that, in its day, was seen by many almost as an excrescence or an intrusion, as antiquated and completely out of step with the predominant "trends," both in its country of origin, Italy, and in the rest of the world. A superfluous work, anachronistic, one that neither "added to" nor "moved things on," as if the history of literature were something that progressed and was, in that respect, akin to science, whose discoveries are left behind or eliminated as they are overtaken or revealed to be incomplete, inadequate or inexact. But literature functions in quite the opposite way: nothing that one adds to it erases or cancels out what came before; rather, it sits alongside those earlier books and coexists with them. Old and new texts breathe in unison, so much so that one wonders sometimes if everything that has ever been written is not simply the same drop of water falling on the same stone, and if, perhaps, the only thing that really changes is the language of each age. The older work still has to "breathe" despite the time that has elapsed since its creation or appearance: and some works—the majority—*are* erased or cancelled out, but this happens of its own accord, not because something else comes along to take their place or to supplant or eject them; rather, they languish and die because of their own lack of spirit or—more precisely—because they aspired to being "modern" or "original," an aspiration that leads inevitably to an early senescence, or, as others might say, they become "dated." "It's very much of its time," we tell ourselves when we read these books in a different, later age, because, given the unstoppable and ever-accelerating speed with which the world moves, "in a different age" can sometimes mean a mere decade later. This is the case even with stories written by some of the great modern authors, such as Kafka, Faulkner, Borges on occasions and Joyce almost always. They can sometimes seem slightly old-fashioned or, if you prefer, dated, precisely because they were so innovative, bold, confident, original and ambitious.

The same cannot be said of Isak Dinesen or of Giuseppe Tomasi di Lampedusa's *The Leopard*. The latter is not in any way an old-fashioned nineteenth-century novel as some critics said at the time, misled perhaps by the century in which the action takes place. It is, without a doubt, a contemporary novel of the kind written by the authors mentioned above, and its author was fully aware of the new techniques and "advances" in the genre, if you can call them that, and was even modest enough to abandon one possibility—that of describing a single day in the life of Prince Fabrizio di Salina— saying: "I don't know how to do a *Ulysses*." But he did know, for example, how to make masterly use of ellipsis, telling a story in fragmentary fashion, unemphatically, even withholding information and leaving unexplained what the reader need only glimpse or intuit, setting up illuminating connections between disparate and apparently secondary or merely anecdotal elements, adroitly bringing together what the characters say and do with what they think (all of which is much more common in the twentieth-century novel than in the novel of the nineteenth century), and, above all, he observes, reflects, suggests and qualifies.

As we know, *The Leopard* was very nearly never published at all, and its author did not live to see it in printed form; indeed, only a few days before his death on 23 July 1957, he received another rejection letter from one of the best Italian publishing houses, which thus added its short-sighted "critical perceptions" to those of another no less prestigious house. More than that, though, *The Leopard* might never have been written at all. Lampedusa was not a writer, and proved to be one only after his death; and he began writing his novel in the last years of his life for, it seems, entirely trivial reasons: the relative late success of his cousin the poet Lucio Piccolo, which led Lampedusa to make the following comment in a letter: "Being absolutely certain that I was no more of a fool than he, I sat down at my desk and wrote a novel"; another reason was his wife, Licy, who encouraged him to write—to write anything, with no pretentions to greatness—simply as a possible way of neutralizing his deep-seated nostalgia; a third reason might have been his solitude: "I am a person," he wrote, "who is very often alone. Of the sixteen hours of daily wakefulness, at least ten are spent in solitude. And being unable, after all, to read the whole time, I amuse myself by constructing literary theories . . ." He did, in fact, spend most of his life reading and, when he went for his daily stroll around the city of Palermo, he always carried a briefcase with him, stuffed with far more books than he could possibly need. He even read (and he read in five or six languages) mediocre, second-rate authors, whom he considered to be as necessary as the literary greats: "One has to learn how to be bored," he said. So there was very little drive and scant ambition behind *The Leopard*. Indeed, as I say, it might never have existed, for Lampedusa himself had doubts about its timeliness and its value. On one occasion, he said to his pupil Francesco Orlando: "It is, I fear, complete rubbish," and he said this, apparently, without false modesty and in good faith. At the same time, though, he believed that it deserved to be published (which is not so very remarkable given how many books—good, mediocre and bad—were published in the twentieth century, not to mention all those that have already been published in the twenty-first century). In "Last wishes of a private person," he wrote: "I would like every effort to be made to publish *The Leopard* . . . this does not mean, of course, that it should be published at the expense of my heirs; I would consider that to be a great humiliation." So while there was little drive and scant ambition when it came to beginning the task, at least there was a certain pride in finishing it.

Lampedusa had good reason to feel proud. *The Leopard* is fresh and bold and free of any of the inhibitions that afflict novelists who feel an undue sense of responsibility towards themselves and their career thus far; it is entirely free of intellectual airs and vanities and of any desire to be original; it has no intention of dazzling or scandalizing or of "opening up new paths"; on re-reading *The Leopard* more than fifty years after it was first published and in another century, it seems to me to be a solitary masterpiece four times over: first, because it is the author's only complete novel; second, because it appeared when he was already dead, and thus stepped out into the world, so to speak, alone; third, because it was the work of an islander cut off from "public" literature until his death; and fourth, because although it never aspired to originality, it is, nonetheless, extraordinarily original. Much has been written about this novel since, and it would be presumptuous of me to attempt to add anything more. We can all agree that it is the preeminent novel about Sicily and about the unification of Italy; that it gives us a portrait of the end of an era and the death of a whole world, as well as a picture of opportunism as embodied in that famous and oft-quoted line: "For everything to remain the same, everything must change"—repeated ad nauseam by those who have never read *The Leopard*—although those words are, in fact, just another fortunate phrase in the book as a whole and incidental to the plot. For me, it is, above all, a novel about death, about one man's preparation for and acceptance of death, even a certain impatience for it to come. Death stalks the book not in any insistent way, but tenuously, respectfully, modestly, almost as part of life and not necessarily the most important part either. Perhaps two of the most moving passages in the book are the Prince of Salina's contemplation of the brief death agony of a hare he has shot during a hunting party, and the final paragraph, in which, almost thirty years after Don Fabrizio himself has died, his daughter Concetta decides to relegate to the rubbish heap the stuffed carcass of a dog that belonged to her father and of whom he was particularly fond, Bendicó.

Of the hare, Lampedusa writes: "Don Fabrizio found himself being stared at by big black eyes soon overlaid by a glaucous veil; they were looking at him with no reproval, but full of tortured amazement at the whole ordering of things; the velvety ears were already cold, the vigorous paws contracting in rhythm, still-living symbol of useless flight; the animal had died tortured by anxious hopes of salvation, imagining it could still escape when it was already caught . . ." And of the dog he writes: "As the carcass was dragged off, the glass eyes stared at her with the humble reproach of things discarded in the hope of final riddance," and this leads the reader to remember another line, much earlier, in which he speaks of the world of Donnafugata as being "deprived thus of that charge of energy which everything in the past continues to possess."

Lampedusa knows that all things take a long time to disappear, that everything takes its time; even something that is already past lingers and resists leaving, even the stuffed carcass of a dog that departed this world decades before. And one can only oppose this slow, inevitable disappearance with a humble, but never rancorous reproach to the order of things. Anyone who knows or senses the existence of this order gradually becomes used to the idea and to the prospect of disappearing, even thinking of it as a "salvation." For example: "He had achieved the portion of death that one can safely introduce into one's existence without renouncing life"; and, elsewhere: "Where there's death there's hope . . ." This doesn't apply solely to places and animals, who do not understand (still less the eyes that are not even eyes, but the glass imitations used by the taxidermist when creating the stuffed version of Bendicò). It applies to people too, most of whom are still unaware and full of life, still convinced that death is something that happens to other people, and yet who are still worthy of compassion. In the famous ball scene, he writes: "The two young people drew away, other couples passed, less handsome, just as moving, each submerged in their passing blindness. Don Fabrizio felt his heart thaw; his disgust gave way to compassion for all these ephemeral beings out to enjoy the tiny ray of light granted them between two shades, before the cradle, after the last spasms. How could one inveigh against those sure to die? . . . Nothing could be decently hated except eternity."

As he says at the end of the sixth chapter: fifty or more years are a mere instant "in the region of perennial certitude." Perhaps it is long enough, though, for all of us still living, still ephemeral novelists—blind, touching figures caught between two shades—to start earning the right to hate *The Leopard*.

(2011)

Writing a Little More

After a more or less obligatory first reading of the great masters of the past, usually in our youth, many of us writers feel somewhat uneasy about revisiting them. It tends to be a rather discouraging, not to say frustrating experience. The novelist or poet picks up a copy of Shakespeare or Cervantes, Montaigne or Hölderlin, Keats or Conrad or Proust, and, after re-reading a few pages, thinks: "What on earth am I doing here at my typewriter or computer? What is the point of me adding a single line to what they have already said?" Re-reading the classics can be an invitation to silence.

I experience this feeling myself with quite a few writers, although not with Shakespeare, who should perhaps be the one author guaranteed to have the most depressing, paralysing effect. Instead, I always find revisiting his work stimulating and enriching. It doesn't invite me to silence at all, but urges me on to write "a little more." How can that be? It would be absurd for anyone to compare himself with Shakespeare, to compete or even slavishly imitate him. One takes his undoubted superiority for granted. Yet far from discouraging me, his work encourages and fills me with a desire to write, and the reason for this is that his texts are so mysterious, even when they appear not to be and seem easy to understand . . . at least initially. There are so many ideas that he merely noted in passing, but left unexplored; as you travel through his plays, you notice so many side streets going off to the left and right that you feel tempted to go down them, to venture off along paths he merely signalled, but did not take, those, so to speak, that he discarded or abandoned.

Seven of my books have titles that quote from or paraphrase Shakespeare: the novels *A Heart So White*, *Tomorrow in the Battle Think on Me*, *Dark Back of Time*, *Your Face Tomorrow* and *Thus Bad Begins*, the volume of stories *When I Was Mortal* and the collection of essays *Seré amado cuando falte* (*I Shall Be Lov'd When I Am Lack'd*). If we look at the lines from *Macbeth* from which the first title comes: "My hands are of your colour; but I shame to wear a heart so white," the meaning of the word "white" is by no means unambiguous. Does it mean "pale" or "cowardly" or "innocent" or "without stain?" If we look at the line from *Hamlet* that I've used as the title for my most recent novel: "Thus bad begins and worse remains behind," the Spanish characters who quote these words take them to mean "and worse is left behind," and yet many Shakespearean exegetes and translators interpret it as meaning "and worse lurks or waits behind" or "worse is yet to come." Shakespeare's ambiguity is there even in some of his most famous and often-repeated lines. We are all familiar with Othello's soliloquy spoken just before he kills Desdemona, which begins thus: "It is the cause, it is the cause, my soul." Almost no one bats an eyelid or pauses when they read or hear this and what follows, and yet it isn't at all clear what Othello is referring to, because he doesn't say "This is the cause" nor, of course, "She is the cause." And what exactly does "In the dark backward and abysm of time" mean, when the word "backward" doesn't even appear to be a noun, strictly speaking? And are Prince Hal's words to his pal Poins any clearer: "What a disgrace is it to me to remember thy name! Or to know thy face tomorrow!" (I, of course, gave this a contradictory twist in my novel *Your Face Tomorrow*.)

The extraordinary thing about Shakespeare is that we don't even notice the often enigmatic nature of his words, which don't get in our way when it comes to "understanding" what we're reading. They don't slow us down, they don't appear cryptic or abstruse. We have a sense that we're capturing everything he says without any difficulty at all. And yet, if you stop and re-read, if you look closely, you often find that while you may have "understood," you haven't entirely "comprehended." The energy, the rhythm, the glow of his images and metaphors, all drive us on, and create in us an illusion of intuition, revelation, or even sudden wisdom. Then, when you emerge from the wave and look back, you realize that there is still much to explore, to develop, to puzzle over and think about. What further encouragement does an author need to write a little more?

(2016)

Roving with a Compass

I'm afraid to say this, but something I lack entirely is any vision of the future. Not only do I not know what I want to write, I don't even know where I want to get to, I don't even have a narrative plan I can propose before or after my novels have been written; indeed, when I begin a novel, I don't even know what it is going to be about, what will happen, or who the characters will be or how many, let alone how it will end. I suppose one of the reasons for this is that, having reached the age of forty and with ten or eleven novels to my name, I feel as if I have passed through at least three very different stages, although this feeling may also be due to the anxiety aroused by my having started to publish very young, when I was only twenty, and to the changes everyone goes through from early youth to maturity.

The fact is that I continue to write rather aimlessly and could never honestly say: "In this novel I was trying to reflect . . ." I envy writers like Balzac and Carlos Fuentes, who both knew what they wanted the totality of their life's work to be. There are others who would not go quite that far, but whom I envy just as much, because, although they restrict themselves to one text at a time, they nevertheless know, right from the start, what they want that book to be and what they intend to write about. They are writers who are, in a way, working with a map, and before they set off, they already know the terrain to be crossed, and off they go, confident that they have the means to reach their goal. On the few occasions when I have mapped out my trajectory beforehand (at most, in the occasional short story), I had the feeling that I was simply writing down what I already knew, which bored me, and boredom is the last thing a writer should feel.

I suppose I work with a compass rather than with a map, and not only do I have no idea what my goal is or what I want to write or what I'm going to write about, I also have no idea about the presentation, to use a term that can cover both what we usually call plot, argument or story as well as the book's formal, stylistic or rhythmic appearance or indeed structure. Feeling one's way forward like that is, I suppose, very dangerous, and usually has catastrophic results. If it has proved to be not quite such a catastrophe in my case, I would like to think this is due to a strange and possibly unnecessary discipline I impose on myself, namely, I do not allow myself to change what I have written as it suits me or as I find out—exactly like the reader—what the novel is about or what is going on; instead, I force myself to be ruled by what I have already written, and allow that to determine what happens next. In a way, I apply to a book the same principle of knowledge that rules life, reality or the world, or whatever you choose to call it: we cannot behave or decide or choose or act according to a known goal or to what might happen later: rather, that goal or subsequent event will have to be ruled by what we have already experienced or known or suffered, none of which can be erased or changed or even forgotten.

This not-knowing allows me to indulge in what I would call roving (although, in my case, I think such roving is only apparent), which, oddly enough, is frowned upon by most critics nowadays, who, doubtless brought up on detective fiction, give great importance to what is "pertinent" or "essential" to the story, as if everything that appears in a narrative should provide useful information that will lead the reader to the inevitable denouement. Barthes talked about *l'effet de réel* to describe the things, details or episodes that happen or occur simply because they do, both in life and in novels, but whose only significance or connection to a story is the one that the author or the reader chooses to find by using his or her associative faculties. Cervantes or Sterne or Proust or, among more modern writers, Nabokov, Bernhard or Benet were masters of that textual roving, or, if you prefer, masters of the digression, the tangent, the aside, the lyrical invocation, the rant and the prolonged autonomous metaphor. None of them, however, could be said to be doing this gratuitously, nor could it be said that their digressions were not "pertinent" or "essential" to the story. Indeed, it is that taste for digression that makes their stories possible.

In my last novel, *A Heart So White*, I discovered (but only once I had finished it) that it was about secrecy and its possible usefulness, about persuasion and instigation, about marriage, about the responsibility that comes with knowing something, the impossibility of knowing anything and the impossibility of not knowing, about suspicion and speaking out and keeping silent. But I only know all this because while I was writing, as happens when reading the authors I mentioned earlier, I found myself obliged to pause for some diversion or digression or aside—my interest as a writer is not very different from my interest as a reader—and, as such, I want to be obliged to stop and think, and while this is happening I really don't mind what the writer is telling me. After all, what is *tellable* in a novel is simply what could also be said in a few, interchangeable words. Novels, however, tend to have a lot of words and those should never be interchangeable.

(1992)

Who Is Who?

When I wrote my novel *All Souls* (1989), I found myself in a situation
entirely new to me as an author, one I had not encountered when writing any of my five previous novels. *All Souls* is set in Oxford, where
I, as narrator and protagonist, had recently spent two years. It was
written in the first person, a first person who, admittedly, bears a
strong resemblance to the "I" in the letters I wrote to my friends in
Spain during my stay in England. The narrator of the novel held the
same post or position that I had held then, and lived in a house identical to the one in which I had lived. Some of the other characters in
the book have *something* in common with people I met in Oxford,
although none is actually "portrayed" in *All Souls*, by which I mean
they are not clearly identifiable. To give one example, the physical
appearance of the character called "Toby Rylands" or "the literary
scholar Toby Rylands" corresponds almost exactly to that of a
retired professor with whom I was on friendly terms during my time
there. However, that is as far as any resemblance goes. The character has some points in common with him and with another old
gentleman whom I was fortunate enough to know during his latter
years, the poet Vicente Aleixandre, but as for what "Toby Rylands"
says (his longest speech in the novel is a monologue he gives during
a conversation he has with the narrator), I can state categorically
that neither the retired Oxford professor nor Vicente Aleixandre

ever said those words: they are as much my own invention as those spoken by any of the characters in my previous novel, *The Man of Feeling* (1986).

I realize that this mingling of things actually experienced and things imagined or invented is not so very unusual; indeed, it is probably the basis of most novels past and present. And yet the experience nonetheless took me by surprise: I had never before had recourse (except in minor details) to anything I had seen or heard or known in order to build a novel on it. I had certainly not done so *knowingly*, and that, of course, was precisely what I had to do in *All Souls*. At the same time, right from the start, I knew that what I was writing *was* a novel and not an autobiographical account or a personal memoir of past events, even when some of the episodes in the novel did approximate to my own experiences. (It should be said that the title of the book in its French translation is *Le Roman d'Oxford*, with the emphasis on the word "novel," and I had considered that same title, *La novela de Oxford*, for the original Spanish version.)

And so when it came to creating my characters, I found that, unlike in my other novels, in which the origin of all the characters had been the same (namely, my imagination), in *All Souls*, the characters had various origins. And even though the way each of them was configured would constitute a unique and isolated case, the characters, as regards origins, were basically of three types, namely: (a) entirely invented characters, as in all my previous novels; (b) a historical character (the writer John Gawsworth); and (c) characters to a greater or lesser extent inspired by, or, rather, to a greater or lesser extent *related* to real people.

I won't comment on the characters in the first category, the most important of whom would be the one called "Clare Bayes," since the only new problem presented by such characters was that of making them fit and blend in on the same undifferentiated plane as those with a different provenance. Nor will I comment on the writer John Gawsworth, since my treatment of him was complex enough to require another essay like this or even a whole book. As for the third group, to which belong the aforementioned "Toby Rylands" and various others, I will focus on the most striking and most problematic one, that of the Narrator, to whom I will also sometimes refer as "the Spaniard," since that is how he is occasionally referred to in the book.

As I say, there were so many similarities (those that can be verified) between the situation of that character and my own that it seemed to me absurd to try to camouflage them. I gave no physical description of him nor did I give him a name (that is, I decided to maintain an ambiguity that would have been impossible had the Narrator said of himself that he had red hair and was six foot three or, on the contrary, had dark hair and was five foot seven; or if he had said that his name was Juan or Pedro or even Javier). In addition, I decided not to create a fictitious or an artificial voice for him, as was the case with the voice of the character called "The Lion of Naples," the narrator of *The Man of Feeling*. Here, I made no attempt to avoid using my own voice, that is, my natural diction when writing, the same voice, for example, in which I had written to friends when I was in England. And yet, even though I was lending my own voice and some of my experiences to that character—the Narrator or the Spaniard—I knew that he wasn't me, but someone different, albeit similar. Or, if you prefer, you could say that the character was "the person I could have been, but wasn't."

I won't deny that, when I began writing *All Souls*, that distinction was not as clear to me as it is now that the book has been finished and published and is out of my hands; and it may be that the opening sentences in the novel express a desire to make clear to myself, right from the start, that problematic distinction:

> But in order to speak of them, I must speak of myself and of my time in the city of Oxford, even though the person speaking is not the same person who was there. He seems to be, but he is not. If I call myself "I," or use a name which has accompanied me since birth and by which some will remember me, if I detail facts that coincide with facts others would attribute to my life, or if I use the term "my house" for the house inhabited by others before and after me but where I lived for two years, it is simply because I prefer to speak in the first person and not because I believe that the faculty of memory alone is any guarantee that a person remains the same in different times and different places. The person recounting here and now what he saw and what happened to him then is not the same person who saw those things and to whom those things happened; neither is he a prolongation of that person, his shadow, his heir or his usurper.

These words, which occur in the very first paragraph, are undeniably part of the novel, since they are placed in the mouth of the Narrator, who will be the person telling us what happens next. And yet it's highly likely that, when they were being written, those words were "still" mine, the author's, and that it was then, through those words, that the author took his leave (or took the opportunity to leave), allowing the Narrator, the Spaniard, to take the floor. Insofar as I can say what I'm about to say, I think that I needed to intervene in my narrator's text that first time so that I could then cease to intervene. In other words, I needed to establish explicitly that difficult separation and to distinguish between "the person now describing what he saw and what happened to him" and "the person who actually saw it and to whom those things did actually happen," and thus deny that they are one and the same. However, I fear that this distinction or differentiation, based on the commonplace idea that none of us is the same all the time except—possibly—as regards memory and name, was not enough for me entirely to take my leave, to exclude myself, Javier Marías, from the text and from the narrative. That is why I added: "neither is he a prolongation of that person, his shadow, his heir or his usurper." This, more than the previous sentence, was my real leave-taking, and granted me the necessary freedom to be able to recount events with the same or customary impunity and impertinence as an entirely fictitious or, as I said before, artificial narrator. Curiously, and possibly quite by chance, those words are true, I think, precisely because it is impossible to know who wrote or is writing them, the Narrator or the author, because they were/are written by them both.

The fact is that once I had established (for myself, the author) that separation or distinction between author and Narrator, I felt free not only to lend the Spaniard my own voice or my usual written style, but also to allow myself to disguise him as me, at least as regards incidental, secondary matters. An example: the Narrator mentions his childhood and recalls how an old nanny used to walk with him and his three brothers down the streets "of Génova or Covarrubias or Miguel Ángel." I do, in fact, have three brothers, I was born in Calle de Covarrubias and spent my early years there, I went to school in Calle de Miguel Ángel and used to go to the cinema in Calle de Génova. The Narrator's birthday is said to be 20 September, which happens to be my birthday too.

This disguise—which I could quite legitimately adopt given the frank disclaimer quoted above, dissociating myself from the Narrator—was, however, after a hundred or so pages, becoming a double-edged sword. The Narrator, whom I earlier defined as some-one who could have been me, was beginning, if I may put it like this, to be unmistakably me, when—or so I thought—with the words "neither is he a prolongation of that person, his shadow, his heir or his usurper," I had made it clear that the Narrator was No One, and could therefore be Anyone. To my way of thinking, the fact that the Narrator was neither my prolongation nor my shadow, my heir or my usurper (nor his) granted the Narrator, right from the start, abso-lute autonomy, so much so that I could allow him to borrow my attributes as well as glimpses of or images from my past without running the risk of me becoming confused with him. It's difficult to be confused with someone who is, in fact, No One. Now, all this was as seen from the point of view of the author, of the person doing the writing, of myself *while* I was writing. From that point of view, the above-mentioned words helped me either to treat myself as a fic-tional character (which would fit that other formula "the person I could have been, but wasn't") or, you might say, to treat a fictional character as if he were me (which would fit the formula "the person who is No One, and yet resembles me"). This new problem arose precisely because of the growing resemblance between this person who was No One, or who quite simply wasn't, and me. And here, the point of view of the author, of the person doing the writing, of me *while* I was writing became relegated to the background. I became aware that, although that point of view was important and vital to how I approached my task as novelist, namely, the execution or creation of the story, it only partially resolved what the reader's perception of that character, the Spaniard, might be. That "declar-ation of principles" given in the first paragraph could be forgotten by the reader and set aside once the story proper had begun, and might, consequently, lack weight, effect and value from the reader's point of view. The biographical note on the jacket stating that the author "taught Spanish literature at the University of Oxford for two years (1983–85)" could lead the reader—and not just a reader who actually knows the author, but an unknown, anonymous reader—to see that initial "declaration" as a mere rhetorical device and to transform me, the author, into the Narrator. Such an assimilation or identification (or a tendency towards that) was and continues to be almost inevitable, but the fact that the Narrator was disguised as me and had many of my characteristics meant that even though the Narrator wasn't me, if he were to be someone, he could only be me, rather than No One or Anyone, or, at the very least, Someone-else-plus-me, as had been my intention. And so, at a given moment, I needed (more from the reader's point of view than the author's) an alibi, something that would allow the Narrator to at least be Someone-else-plus-me, or, in other words, not necessarily me (by which I mean a fictitious "I," but not necessarily *that* fictitious "I").

My chosen method was extremely simple, although the path leading to it was not. I simply had to attribute to the Narrator a circumstance or event that bore no possible relation to me as the author. At one point, the Narrator states that after his two-year stay in Oxford, and back in his own city of Madrid, he is now married and has a child, who is only a few months old at the time of writing. I have never been married and have no children, and that is the only verifiable fact that prevents or could prevent a complete identification between the Narrator and the author that any reader—be he friend or relative or anonymous stranger—might try to establish. That verifiable fact, I should add, gave me even greater freedom when it came to emphasizing any similarities between the Narrator and me, without that fact, or so I thought, destroying the deliberate ambiguity I had opted for in not giving the Narrator a name or any physical description, because there is, in my view, a substantial difference between that second option (stating that the Narrator is married and has a child) and the option I rejected from the start (the Narrator is very tall and has red hair or the Narrator's name is Juan), and the difference lies in the fact that I, the author, could never have red hair and be six foot three tall, or be called Juan (given that my name is Javier), while I, the author, could well have got married and had a child on my return from the city of Oxford. By using that very simple subterfuge (which was not merely a subterfuge, but essential to the plot), the Narrator could continue to accumulate as many characteristics or elements of the author's disguise as I wished without that necessary ambiguity being in any way lost. In short, he could, in the novel as a whole, be "the person I could have been, but wasn't" as well as "the person who is No One, and yet resembles me" and, finally—or so I would like to think—he could also be No One or Anyone, or, at the very least, Someone-else-plus-me.

(1990)

Time Machines

More and more people are astonished when they see or find out that I still write using an electric typewriter, as if such machines were ancient relics. Not just because almost all my colleagues have long since moved on to computers, but also because, according to what many of my readers say, "they can tell" that I write on one of those machines with the greenish or bluish screens, on which, it seems, you have only to press a key to find out instantaneously where and how often you have used the words "memory" or "frying pan." In my most recent novels, there is what I call a system of echoes and resonances, whereby phrases that seem, at first, to be merely trivial and of no particular significance reappear many pages later, sometimes identical but in a different context, sometimes with variations, like musical motifs, and thus they take on a deeper meaning or turn out not to be insignificant at all, but to form an essential part of the story. And the only possible explanation, it seems, is the computer's memory, as if our own faculties were incapable of such feats and were slowly atrophying.

I don't think I could achieve the same thing (always assuming that I have) were I to liberate my memory from the tension needed to recover and reincorporate those repeated phrases or images. If I knew that I had only to press a key in order to summon up what I had written months before without myself making any effort to bring it back, I might well not even consider doing it, I might not make the same connections or maintain that same degree of alertness, I might become oblivious to the internal links in the novel. The fact that a machine can perform a particular function for us does not mean that it will. Indeed, the permanent possibility of being able to do something can have a dissuasive or even preventative effect. A similar thing is happening with home videos, where the filming and accumulating and filing away of certain scenes means that many people no longer recall them. Knowing that they are there, with every movement reproduced in real time, along with every gesture we made and the exact words we spoke, knowing that we can "relive" them whenever we want to means that we are more likely to forget them. Their perpetual availability is an invitation to ignore them.

There are a few other reasons too why I haven't started using a computer and probably never will. One of those reasons is that what I enjoy about writing is the time it takes. I enjoy taking the sheet of paper out of the machine once I've typed it, reading it through, then crossing things out and shifting them around, making changes I can see and that don't disappear for good once I've made them, because I often go back to what I've crossed out and reinstate it, deciding that what I thought was bad at one stage in the process is, in fact, good. You can always find those changes if you have the various drafts before you. And although I realize that you can also print things off from a computer, I don't know anyone who does print off each and every one of the versions that he or she will later discard and that will never be seen by the reader. Another reason is that, according to computer converts, once you've tried writing on a computer, you can't write on anything else, which, if it's true, seems to me disastrous and highly dangerous, since you won't, I imagine, always have your computer to hand. And there are those—for example, that very intelligent American critic Edward Mendelson—who maintain that the computer affects and impoverishes the rhythm of the prose, that the mechanical ease of writing leads authors to write in a more uniform fashion, with more monotonous sentences all of the same length. That seems rather unlikely to me, but I add it as a last resort, like a cat lying belly up on the carpet.

I have to admit, though, that my main reason is an aesthetic one: right now, those little screens have an exaggeratedly modern air, whereas most of us writers look distinctly *démodé*. I've seen many photos of novelists sporting beards straight out of the nineteenth century or Trotsky-style spectacles or Isadora Duncan scarves or long Cossack overcoats or Becquerian hairdos, and there they are posing next to one of those aseptic, refined contraptions; the result is frankly painful and off-putting in the extreme: they look like anxious, unwitting time-travellers; it's rather like seeing Valle-Inclán dressed up as the Terminator or, worse still, as Robocop.* And so I prefer to remain entirely antiquated, my life being quite full enough of contradictions.

(1995)

---

* Ramón María del Valle-Inclán (1866–1936) was a Spanish writer whose image is indelibly etched in literary consciousness through many portraits, illustrations and photographs: he always sported round spectacles, long hair and a very long and somewhat unkempt beard, black at first, then greying and white as he grew older.

The Isolated Writer

I think most writers tend to feel isolated or, indeed, want to be isolated, especially after a certain age. Perhaps this isn't the case initially, particularly among those who start writing and publishing young. In one's early years, it's exciting to belong to a new and supposedly innovative group or generation. We often despise our immediate predecessors, notably those who come from the same country as ourselves and write in the same language. We judge them to be wrong, out of step, old-fashioned, we have no sympathy for them and are in a hurry to dismiss them. We often, quite unfairly, deny that they have any worth at all and consider them a mere mistake in the history of literature, destined soon to be forgotten. Young writers jump over their literary parents and "reclaim" their grandparents, who, to them, seem weak, unthreatening and on the retreat. However, this feeling of camaraderie and combat, of being part of "a new wave," is short-lived. As soon as a writer stops looking at the other writers around him, he ceases to be concerned about the "state" or "future" of literature in his own country and language, realizing that this is what matters least to him and that, besides, it is not his responsibility. Instead, he devotes himself to the one thing he should devote himself to, namely, writing his own books as if there were no other books in the world, and it is then that he begins to feel isolated. This is partly of his own choosing and partly because he has no alternative if he is to continue as a writer.

This is not, of course, merely the well-known—and very real—solitude in which all writers work and about which much has been said. It is simply the way in which the novelist chooses to spend his days—the novelist more than the poet, the dramatist or even the essayist—just as others choose or are obliged to spend their days in an office or a factory, permanently surrounded by people. It is, more than anything, the need to feel *almost* unique, rather than the mere interchangeable member of a generation or group, rather than even "a child of one's time." Nothing irritates a real writer more than those critics, professors and cultural commentators who insist on labelling him or setting him in context or establishing links between his work and that of his contemporaries, in attributing to him membership of certain trends or movements or fashions, in describing him as "realistic" or "historical" or as "a literary writer"—that absurd tautology that has become so popular in our own stupid age—or as a cultivator of "autofiction"—another ridiculous concept currently in vogue—or as a "postmodernist writer"—I've never known what that adjective means, but it is, fortunately, falling into disuse. The real writer is also infuriated by attempts to establish "his place" in the literary tradition of his country and language or to find connections between him, that tradition and its classic works. The writer knows that the country in which he was born and the language in which he writes, while important, are only secondary, even, up to a point, accidental, fortuitous and reversible. He knows that Proust could have existed in Italian or English, Lampedusa in Spanish or German, Thomas Mann in Czech or Swedish, or Cervantes, even, in French or Portuguese: he knows that language is just a vehicle, a tool, never an end in itself or something sacred, and not in any way superior to those who use it. It is not a determining factor, or perhaps only in certain "ornamental" writers, who, in Spanish, for example, seem to expect their readers to cry "Olé!" after each exquisite, elegant, quintessentially Castilian phrase. It makes little difference if a writer shares the same language as Shakespeare or Dante, Montaigne or Hölderlin, Conrad or Nabokov or Wittgenstein, still less when one remembers that the last three writers all switched languages at some point in their lives and chose the language in which they wanted to express themselves.

All these things annoy the writer, and quite rightly so, because he will only manage to write and finish what he is writing if he works in the false belief that his book is the only book in the world. If he looks up from his typewriter or his computer—I still use a typewriter—if he glances back at the past or into the future and sees his work reduced to just another name on an endless list; or if he looks at the present and wastes time wondering how his colleagues are getting on, what they're up to and what they have achieved and how original or profound they are; or if he considers his predecessors or, indeed, allows himself to be overwhelmed by all the marvellous things that have been written before and that will doubtless be written after his uncertain passage through the world, he will be lost. That is why a writer needs to isolate himself *while* he is writing, and, needless to say, *only* while he is writing. He knows full well that his false belief is, as I said, both false and transient. He knows that once the book he has written has left his room and has been exposed to other eyes and, finally, published, it will disappear among hundreds of thousands of other books, and he will see it then as just another drop in the ocean, which, like all the other drops, will be doing its best to be noticed. He will have the sense that his book is, if anything, superfluous.

Besides, no writer nowadays can take much comfort in the idea of posterity, seeking refuge in some far-off future, trusting that time and its mysterious selection process will single him out as special on some distant day that he will not even be around to see. There always was something slightly ridiculous and somewhat pathetic about the idea of posterity. Now it seems positively grotesque, given that the "lifetime" of things is becoming ever shorter, a process that is happening at an ever more dizzying speed; the release of a film, a piece of music or a book instantly transforms them into "something that has been and gone"; we have the impression that the only things that truly exist are those that do not yet exist, but are about to, and the mere existence of something—the film you can already see, the music you can already hear, the book you can already read—signals its imminent expiry and immediately relegates it to the past. We have already seen or heard or read that work, we want something new, which means, of course, that we are always waiting. It's as if the idea of durability belonged to another age entirely, and is, therefore, only within the grasp of those—Shakespeare, Montaigne, Cervantes, even Conrad and Nabokov—who achieved it when such an idea was still conceivable, still possible. As if it were no longer achievable by any writers living now. For a writer nowadays to think that he will be remembered is entirely at odds with the workings of the modern world, in which everything is "old" the moment it has been born; it is quite simply incompatible with everything around us; it is, in short, grotesque, and this only adds to a writer's sense of isolation and transience. One thinks: "I only really exist *while* I'm writing, that is, as long as no one can see me and as long as no one knows what I'm doing. Paradoxically, I exist only as long as my work and I remain hidden, as long as we do not as yet exist for the world. As soon as we appear, we will cease to exist and become lost among the swift, impatient rabble that devours, digests and excretes everything." Emily Dickinson wrote: "Publication is the auction of the mind of man," and that is an idea I often return to. It is the vile contact with the external world, with the crowd, with the millions of pages similar to our own, all born of the same impulse. It is finding ourselves placed in the framework of a tradition, be it of our own country, our own language or of the whole history of literature (doubtless as a footnote). It is the realization that, far from being unique, we have a great deal in common with our predecessors and with our contemporaries; the realization that the former, whom we have possibly never even read, did the same as we did, only years before, and that the latter, who do not even know us and are unaware of our existence, write books that are, irritatingly enough, connected to our own. It is at this painful moment that we are obliged to accept that such a thing as a zeitgeist does exist, and that we are, involuntarily and unconsciously, at its service.

Occasionally, there is an even stronger reminder that we are just one more name to be added to the many others, that we are part of a list. This occasion is one such reminder—one, however, that comes in the most pleasant of guises. I have received various prizes (most of them foreign, few of them Spanish), but I don't believe I have ever before been honoured with one as long-standing as this Austrian State Prize for European Literature, which, I see from the list, was first awarded in 1965. On that list are writers whom I admired when I was very young—when I was only a reader and not even a secret writer—and who seem to have had time enough to achieve posterity, for they lived in an age in which the concept was allowed: names like that of the great poet Auden and the dramatist Ionesco, the magnificent Italo Calvino and Simone de Beauvoir, Dürrenmatt and Manganelli. These were figures whom I viewed almost as extraterrestrial beings, some ever since I was a child, and who, I was sure, bore no resemblance to myself, being unsurpassable, given their greater age and artistic achievement. There are other admirable names on the list as well, those of writers who are still alive or only recently dead and who belong, therefore, to the confused, forgetful, swift-flowing times in which we live: Kundera and Rushdie, Esterházy and Lobo Antunes, Eco and Semprún, Barnes and Enquist and Magris. I have even met some of them briefly, but—how can I put it—for me, they have always been "them," "the others," the writers I read and from whom I feel quite separate. And so, in receiving this Austrian State Prize for European Literature, I cannot but feel puzzled (as well as grateful) to see my name added to a list that makes me somehow less myself, that makes me exist less. Or perhaps, who knows, it makes me exist more, when, as now, I am not shut up in my room, or hidden away, tapping at my old, anachronistic typewriter (or playing "at home with paper like a child," as Stevenson put it). How can I possibly believe that my books are isolated, when I am shown with such kindness and clarity that, on the contrary, whether I like it or not, they form part of a long and noble chain called European literature. Thank you very much.

(2011)

Too Much Snow

Those who have read my novels *All Souls* and *Dark Back of Time* will be familiar with the name John Gawsworth, the second King of Redonda, John I, although others will certainly not. Suffice it to say that what initially drew me to Gawsworth, who was born in 1912 and died in 1970, was the enormous contrast between his beginning and his end. He started out as a precocious, promising young author, first published when he was only nineteen, became the youngest member of the Royal Society of Literature, was twice or perhaps thrice married, and was created monarch of the real and fictitious and eminently literary Realm of Redonda (an island next to those two tourist hot-spots, the islands of Montserrat and Antigua), and yet he ended his days as a beggar, at the age of fifty-eight.

One of those strange, altruistic English literary societies, The Friends of Arthur Machen, unearthed and issued, on DVD, part of a BBC film shown just two and a half months before Gawsworth's death in hospital. Two years before that, for lack of funds, the poet had been obliged to leave his last fixed address: a rented room in Bayswater. After that, he became what we would now call "a home-less person," and when his patient friends or his last girlfriend were unable or unwilling to give him shelter, he had no option but to sleep rough on some bench in Hyde Park. An appeal was set up to help him, and this aroused the interest of the BBC, who, in early 1970, made a brief, somewhat charmless documentary featuring Gawsworth himself and some of his old friends, Lawrence Durrell being the best known.

When you have become accustomed to thinking of someone not so much as a flesh-and-blood person, but more as a fictitious character, it is a somewhat unreal experience to hear them speak and see them move—and in colour too. I, of course, knew that Gawsworth really did exist, but had incorporated him into my novels as one of my characters, and his story, of which for a long time I knew only snippets, seemed more like a Kipling tale than real life. In the DVD, Gawsworth is nearing the end. According to Barry Humphries's commentary at the beginning, "John Gawsworth has been, as a literary personality, corroded by something which has afflicted many other artists, greater and lesser than himself. He has, more than anyone else I know, espoused failure—with perhaps too much affection." On the day of filming, though, Gawsworth had clearly taken special pains over his appearance, insofar as he could. Dressed in double-breasted suit and tie and raincoat (and looking rather like an unemployed civil servant), we see him striding along the streets of his native London with his walking stick, which he doubtless needs as a support, but with which he is also capable of making the occasional graceful flourish, reminiscent of his days as a skilled swordsman. His brown shoes are not too old and shabby, and he has clearly polished them for the occasion. Somewhat on the plump side, he is still pretty quick on his feet, and although his face is rather puffy—possibly due to the alcohol that was his ruin and the cause of his various ills—his bright eyes and large nose give him an alert, almost foxlike air, an impression accentuated by his gingerish moustache, much lighter in colour than his hair; who knows, perhaps it was dyed. His nose is quite remarkable. Describing it as large could give rise to confusion, because although it was indeed large, as well as having a strange kink in it, it was long rather than broad.

His friends look slightly uncomfortable, but seem perfectly happy to talk about him. Durrell, who, after his *Alexandria Quartet*, had espoused *success* with perhaps too much affection, speaks of him with a mixture of genuine esteem and unwitting condescension, and is at his most unconvincing when he greets Gawsworth in a pub with a cry of "Hail, O King! Hail, O King!" as if he were fulfilling some kind of melancholy duty. The novelist Kate O'Brien receives him in her house, which is the scene of the one humorous episode in the whole documentary, when Gawsworth struggles manfully to extract the cork from a small bottle of sparkling wine, before passing it to the lady for her to have a go, with an equal lack of success ("We've never been defeated by a bottle, Kate, you or I," Gawsworth says); she returns it to him and, after considerable effort, he finally manages to uncork it. On a visit to a publisher's where he worked years before, he is greeted by an executive, who chats with him stiffly and is clearly anxious for him to leave. Shortly before the end, the poet's voice off-screen is heard describing his painful situation: "Now I haven't an address, you see . . . Until I have an address, I can't collect my books, papers or anything." And that is that. The final image shows him walking through a snow-covered park, his walking stick in his right hand and his left hand casually thrust in the pocket, not of his raincoat, which he wears jauntily unbuttoned, but of his jacket, as if he were Cary Grant. When he reaches a bench, he sits down on it and places both hands on the head of his walking stick. The image freezes, and one only hopes that he did not have to spend the night there when the production team and the camera crew left—not with all that snow around.

(2006)

The Much-Persecuted Spirit of Joseph Conrad

A few weeks ago, I received from a second-hand bookseller a pamphlet written by Joseph Conrad's widow and published by the Mark Twain Society in 1932. Conrad married late, when he was thirty-eight and Jessie was just twenty-three. This fact (plus Conrad's grey beard) doubtless explains why, day after day, during their honeymoon on the French coast, a fellow guest at the hotel where they were staying, a young man who sat next to the young bride during meals at the long, communal table, proved rather too attentive, arousing the suspicions of the writer and causing great embarrassment to his wife. Finally, the Frenchman went up to Conrad and asked with a bow: "Sir, may I have the honour of paying my attentions to your daughter?" This was the first time that Jessie Conrad had to restrain her husband from fighting a duel on the spot. Judging by the two books she wrote about him after his death, it is clear that she was a sensible woman with a sense of humour and that she loved him very much.

In this rare pamphlet, she explains her great admiration for Sir Conan Doyle, but says that it would have been far greater had the creator of Sherlock Holmes not sent her a troubling letter in 1929. (It is well known, and a great shame, that in his latter years—he died in 1930—this fine writer embraced occultism and spiritualism and,

as can be seen from what follows, must have become a real bore.)
Despite never having had any previous contact with Mrs. Conrad,
Conan Doyle wrote to tell her that he was convinced that her late
husband—Conrad died in 1924—wanted to get in touch with her,
warning that this was not easy for the dead without the help of the
living, since the dead remain as subject to laws as we are. According
to him, Conrad had "got his chance at Mrs. Dean's" (presumably a
medium) and "put his face upon the plate," which, it must be said,
sounds rather ghoulish. Later, Sir Arthur went on, he had a sitting
"with Van Reuter and his mother," who knew nothing about Conrad. The latter, through the medium (it's not clear whether this was
Van Reuter or his mother), had expressed his wish that Conan Doyle
should complete a book "about French history" which he himself had
left unfinished: "None of us knew that there was such a book. On
inquiry I found that it was so, but apparently it had been finished by
someone else. So I did no more." According to Jessie, Sir Arthur was
misinformed; not only had Conrad never thought of writing on such
a vague topic, he would certainly never have asked someone else to
complete a book that he had begun, not even a famous colleague.
The worst came last: "It is your duty to go to a good medium and
give him a chance," he said and proceeded to give her a number of
addresses of gifted mediums.

Jessie Conrad adds that, later, another three people tried to pass
on "messages" from her husband, all of which she flatly declined to
receive. More than that, Lord Northcliffe's secretary published a
statement that the author of *Heart of Darkness* was helping his late
boss with some newspaper work and that both men were wearing grey
flannel suits and red bow ties. "My husband," comments Jessie, "was
blessed with sufficient personal vanity to have realized that he could
not venture to copy his lordship's style of dress, in this particular, at

least!" And a niece of the American writer Stephen Crane, who died in 1900, declared that her uncle and Conrad had met in mid-ocean only a few hours after Conrad had died.

The most that Jessie Conrad will admit, as regards such "phenomena," is that sometimes, alone in her room, she spent many an hour with her mind concentrated upon the memory of her husband, with her eyes fixed upon his favourite chair, and that during those moments of intense concentration, his form in complete contour occupied that chair. "The long familiar pose, the play of the well known features, the clasped hands were exactly as I so well remember them. This vision has lasted several seconds. I cannot explain it, and I don't think I would try, except that such a manifestation was for me alone." I would say that there is nothing so very unusual about this; memories can sometimes be very vivid. And at the end of the pamphlet, she concludes very sensibly: "I would so much rather be left to my original belief that those whom we love and have lost are at rest and in peace, untroubled by any law . . . and without being called upon to suffer by their knowledge of the pain and trouble of us still in the land of the living."

(2006)

The Improbable Ghost of
Juan Benet

A few days after receiving the strange pamphlet in which Joseph Conrad's widow described how Conan Doyle had pestered her about her husband's supposed attempts to get in touch, I received a letter from Puerto Rico sent by a kind reader and teacher whom I had met a few months earlier in Madrid. This sensible and highly educated lady apologized in advance for what she was about to tell me ("I am less concerned about what you might think of me than I am about troubling or inconveniencing you in any way"). She was not, she said, a religious person, but a rationalist and something of a sceptic, although she confessed that in recent years she had felt a certain curiosity about "spiritual matters," and so, once a month, she met up with a female Cuban psychologist "who seems to have spiritual powers." Anyway, when she mentioned our meeting to this psychologist, the latter immediately "closed her eyes, apparently went into some kind of trance and announced that someone you had loved very much was there, that the spirit's name was Benet and had chosen to appear in order to get in touch with you. She added that she could see Benet 'tousling the long hair of a young man' and that you were that young man. She said that this was something Benet would do whenever you were feeling sad or pessimistic." (I should perhaps say that between 1970 and 1974, the first years of my friendship with the writer Juan Benet, I did wear my hair long, Apache style, if you like, as certain photographs can testify.)

My correspondent was left speechless and went away "feeling stunned." She couldn't stop thinking about this incident and so decided to talk to a woman friend of hers, who was also a psychologist and who also "appears to have spiritual powers, although it is something she resists." They met and, as soon as they began talking, her friend told her that Benet was there and was asking her to intercede in order to help my "incarnate soul"; and she heard the words "There is no need to speak, no need to do" and "To do without doing." Then she added that "Benet was a wise man, endowed, it would seem, with a great sense of humour because, before leaving, he genuflected." The teacher was astonished, and at her second meeting with the psychologist, the latter told her that "Benet was there and wished you to know that he had appeared and wanted to help you. He added that he had been very sad to die because he was leaving you, a person he had greatly loved and who had been very important in his life." My correspondent apologized again ("I am sending you this letter anyway, in the belief that this is what I should do") and signed off. Her letter, of course, bears no resemblance to the almost impertinent insistence of the great Sir Arthur Conan Doyle in his letter to the grieving Jessie Conrad.

On 5 January 2007, it will be fourteen years since the death of Juan Benet, from whom I learned many things, not only in the field of literature, and with whom I was friends for more than two decades. Oddly enough, it has been his detractors who have ensured that he has not been forgotten as a writer. During all this time, many of his colleagues and mine have continued and continue to rail against him. Idiocy and temerity often go hand in hand, and these critics are themselves, funnily enough, risible as writers, people like Ussía or Sánchez Dragó, or, like some of the newer coarse arrivals on the scene, hypocritical and cowardly, and who, I can only assume, hide their renowned "wit" where the sun don't shine, because it's very hard to spot. Since they're not bright enough to understand Benet, they have decided that he counted for nothing and that no one has read him. In that case, why are they so angry with him, when he hasn't published a line or trodden this earth for nearly fifteen years now? His shadow must make them feel terribly inadequate. His books aren't easy and I wouldn't criticize anyone who found them daunting. However, given that the dim and the dull-witted continue to bark at him, those books must still be alive and kicking, and they are the only way in which he is still "in touch," at least the only way worth mentioning.

What I do not believe is that his spirit has appeared to a couple of female psychologists in Puerto Rico. Like Conrad's sensible widow, I believe that "those whom we love and have lost are at rest and in peace, untroubled by any law." And I don't believe in the improbable either. Jessie Conrad could not imagine her husband asking Conan Doyle to complete a book he himself had left unfinished or wearing a red bow tie in imitation of Lord Northcliffe, and while I can imagine Benet jokily genuflecting, I certainly cannot imagine him making such twee or sentimental remarks, far less declaring how important I had been in his life. As I wrote to my correspondent, he was important in my life, but I wasn't important in his at all. I don't believe in apparitions or messages from beyond the grave (apart from in ghost stories and in dreams, which are, just that, pleasant dreams and stories), but if someone comes to me with the tale that some celebrated dead person is out there stalking me, the very least I would ask is that he continue to speak as he did when alive and not go around uttering the kind of portentous nonsense that would never have sullied his lips in life.

(2006)

THOSE WHO ARE STILL HERE

The Hero's Dreadful Fate

However much certain optimists may talk about the survival or possible resurrection of the Western, I fear—much to my regret—that, as a genre, it is pretty much dead and buried, a relic of a more credulous, more innocent, more emotional age, an age less crushed or suffocated by the ghastly plague of political correctness. Nonetheless, whenever a new Western comes out, I dutifully go and see it, albeit with little expectation that it will be any good. In the last decade, I can recall three pointless remakes, vastly inferior to the films on which they were modelled and which weren't exactly masterpieces themselves: *3:10 to Yuma* by James Mangold, *The Alamo* by John Lee Hancock, and *True Grit* by the Coen brothers, all of them uninspired and unconvincing, and far less inspired than the distinctly uneven originals made, respectively, by Delmer Daves, John Wayne and Henry Hathaway. I recall, too, Andrew Dominik's interesting but dull *The Assassination of Jesse James by the Coward Robert Ford*, Ed Harris's bland, soulless *Appaloosa*, David Von Ancken's unbearable *Seraphim Falls*, and the Australian John Hillcoat's *The Proposition*, of which my memory has retained not a single image. The only recent Westerns that have managed to arouse my enthusiasm have been those made for TV: Walter Hill's *Broken Trail* and *Deadwood*; and the fact that no one has even bothered to bring out the third and final season of the latter on DVD in Spain will give you some idea of how unsuccessful the magnificent first two series must have been. In my view, Kevin Costner's *Open Range*, which came out slightly earlier, was the last decent Western to be made for the big screen, even though it has long been fashionable to denigrate anything this admirable actor and director does.

What has happened to bring about the sad demise of a genre that produced many masterpieces in the past, as well as other fine or worthy films? Nowadays, the few who take up the genre do so either on a whim or out of affectation or in a pompous or archaeological spirit, and the films they make lack naturalness, freshness and that very necessary touch of ingenuousness. In other words, they don't believe in the story they're telling and showing us, they don't dare to; the epic strikes them as old-fashioned, ridiculous, even embarrassing, and, absurdly enough, they seem uncomfortable with the potential complexity of their characters and their stories. I say "absurdly" because the Western has given us some of the most complex characters and stories in the history of cinema. John Ford is just as "deep" as Orson Welles—who greatly admired Ford—or Anthony Mann or Bergman, or, of course, Peckinpah, and certainly as deep as those two overrated charlatans Lars von Trier and Alejandro González Iñárritu.

Perhaps it's because the Western, as a genre, has traditionally embodied attitudes and behaviour—which it always took seriously, without ever falling into caricature—that now seem shocking to the hypocritical mass of entrenched goody-goodies, who desperately want to dissociate themselves from a whole range of passions that have been common to humanity throughout the ages. For example, in the Western, nobody looks askance at hatred, ambition, the desire for revenge, the determined pursuit of an enemy, the wish to hurt or kill that enemy, the search for redress and sometimes justice for a wrong committed. Take the character played by James Stewart in the Anthony Mann films *Winchester '73* and *The Man from Laramie* (purely as examples and because neither film is particularly violent or heartless): he is capable of giving up everything and dedicating himself body and soul to hunting down those who killed his father (in the first film) and his younger brother (in the latter). In the first film, Lin McAdam's sole occupation is the relentless pursuit—across half of the West—of an individual named Dutch Henry Brown, who shot McAdam's father in the back and who turns out, in the end, to be McAdam's own brother. The second character, Will Lockhart, stays on in the remote, unfriendly town of Coronado precisely because he has been insulted, lassoed and dragged through the dust and because he suspects that someone from the town was responsible for selling the repeating rifles with which the Apaches ambushed and killed his younger brother, a soldier in the cavalry. That is all that matters to McAdam and Lockhart; what remains of their life—if there is anything—is put on hold by the one goal they care about. Characters in Westerns never have a future; indeed, they fear that, once their mission has been accomplished, they will be confronted by that uncomfortable notion: the future, a notion without which most people nowadays cannot live and to which we are all indebted and enslaved. Perhaps that is why Westerns tend to avoid or conceal that phase, ending when the protagonist has done what he feels he had to do, thus sparing us that horrible moment when he raises his head, looks around him and, as if emerging from a dream, asks himself: "Now what? I didn't die in the attempt, so what shall I do with the rest of my life?"

One of the best films ever made, John Ford's *The Man Who Shot Liberty Valance*, doesn't show us that future life either, but it forces us to imagine it. It is a Western that marks a milestone in the history of the genre, for various reasons, and not just those I have mentioned already, and which I will discuss later. It contains a brief treatise on politics, a Shakespearean dissertation on freedom of expression and freedom of choice, and a clear ethical dilemma. The protagonist, Ransom Stoddard, again played by James Stewart, is a lawyer from the East, who is shocked and horrified by the brutality of the bandit Liberty Valance, by the impunity in which he lives (for he is protected by the big ranchers who occasionally hire him), and by the fear he inspires in the population of Shinbone, another one-horse town in which Stewart chooses to settle, again because that is where he was attacked and beaten, this time with a whip handle. He, however, intends to use the law to bring Valance to justice and to prison, an ambition that meets with general ridicule and fear. (Those who already know the story, please bear with me.) The John Wayne character, Tom Doniphon (whose tale is one of the saddest I have ever heard), warns him from the start that he should get a gun and learn how to use it, because there is no law in Shinbone and no justice worthy of the name. Stewart resists, but, in the end, against all probability and against all the odds, he kills Liberty Valance in an apparently unequal duel: the boastful, much-feared, expert gunman falls to the ground before a man in a kitchen apron who has never shot anyone in his life. Later, when Stewart refuses to accept a political nomination—the beginning of a long career that will eventually take him all the way to the Senate—because his fame is based on a violent crime that goes against all his principles, John Wayne explains what really happened. He had been hiding down an alleyway, and he, not Stewart, had killed Valance with his rifle, which he fired at the exact moment that Stewart unleashed his one wildly inaccurate shot. Stewart expresses his amazement and asks why he did it, why he saved his life, thus condemning himself to losing the woman he loves, Hallie, who had realized that same night, when she saw Stewart close to death, that *he* was the man she loved. Wayne replies soberly (no other actor could express so much with a simple glance, in this and other films): "Cold-blooded murder? I can live with that." What better summation of the profundity and complexity so often found in Westerns: they understand that not all men are the same, that some are capable of living with certain actions, their own or someone else's (the Stewart character, of course, is not); that some care nothing about the future, even if it exists, as is the case with Tom Doniphon, who wanted Hallie's happiness above all else, even if that meant destroying his own chance of happiness, and to do that, he murdered a man in cold blood, thus allowing the survival of the man Hallie would then marry (Hallie, it should be said, in Vera Miles's memorable portrayal, is one of John Ford's most touching creations, and that's saying a lot).

The film begins and ends many years after these events, with Wayne's funeral, to which a much older Stoddard, now Senator Stoddard, and his wife, Hallie, travel from Washington. The journalists in Shinbone, who want to know why such an important politician has travelled all the way to this godforsaken place in the West merely to attend a funeral, ask initially: "Who's dead?" They don't even know. And when they are told the name, Tom Doniphon, they have no idea who he is. As I said before, the alert viewer is forced to imagine Doniphon's long years of solitude and obscurity on his little ranch on the outskirts of town, alone apart from his faithful black servant, Pompey, and watching the decades pass with no hope and no change—his fate fixed forever—doubtless trapped in the memory of that far-off night when he committed a cold-blooded murder (of a vile individual, it's true; "A murder. Nothing more," as the musketeer Athos once said), and one that worked entirely to his disadvantage. It is one of the few Westerns in which we are obliged to imagine the hero's dreadful future—once he has done the deed, once he has made his choice.

Our society does not accept that all men and all women are different. It does not accept that while some are horrified by what they are obliged or choose to do, others are not, and are prepared to bear whatever responsibility or sentence falls to them. It believes, rather, that everyone should think the same or at least abstain from doing what the majority deem reprehensible. It does not accept that some crimes are not as criminal as others, depending on who commits them and against whom, depending, too, on why. Society knows all about hatred, envy and revenge, but prefers to clothe itself in virtue and pretend ignorance, and, for that reason, it hates not only those who do not pretend and thus remind society of the truth about its past, but also those who harbour an undying hatred or choose to take justice into their own hands. And in the latter case, there's no denying that they're right. "This isn't the Wild West," people say. Fortunately so. But perhaps we live in an age so pusillanimous that it cannot even tolerate serious stories from another age, when men were less respectful of the law and less obedient and less fair, but also more complex, more contradictory and more profound.

(2011)

Riding Time

Critics—as those of the literary variety have been demonstrating for centuries now—have a limitless ability to get things wrong; among the literary critics' horrendous gaffes—to give just one out of thousands of possible examples, examples that are ever on the increase—was the almost unanimous drubbing they gave to Herman Melville's *Moby-Dick* when it was first published. Film critics have only had a little over a hundred years to prove their ignorance and bad taste and general dimwittedness, but in that brief space of time they have already succeeded in reaching the depths plumbed by their literary colleagues. (Of course there are always exceptions, but they are just that, exceptions.) Critics have the advantage that, after a few decades, when a work they praised to the skies has been completely forgotten and one they denigrated is alive and well and deemed to be a classic, almost no one remembers what they said about it; and since they never lack for cheek, they're more than capable of pretending that they didn't say what they said and leaping aboard whichever bandwagon happens to be fashionable at the time.

Nowadays, everyone—apart from the occasional conceited Spanish director—considers *The Searchers* (1956) to be not only one of John Ford's greatest masterpieces, but one of the best films in the history of cinema. That wasn't always the case. Initially, it was judged to be weak and flawed, then it was relegated to a prolonged spell in oblivion, and then it was dismissed as "racist" (yes, there are still people who confuse a film or book with what its characters do and say). Only relatively recently, thanks to a handful of stubborn critics and a far larger number of fans who had been right all along, has this marvellous film found its rightful place in the canon.

The same has not yet happened, however, with another John Ford film made only five years later and closely related to *The Searchers*: *Two Rode Together*, which is still considered by many to be weak and flawed and, of course, a lesser work in comparison with its predecessor. Well, it's true that it is fourteen minutes shorter, that the plot is rather simpler and the script less daring, that the action takes place over a period of a few weeks, not five years or more, and that, for all those reasons, it is perhaps less epic. I suppose it's actually a sourer, sadder, more cynical and more pessimistic version of the story told in *The Searchers* and it does leave a somewhat bitter taste in the mouth. In *The Searchers*, Ethan Edwards (John Wayne) sets off in search of his nieces immediately after they have been abducted by the Comanches. He soon learns that the older girl has been raped and murdered, but this knowledge only drives him on in his search for the younger niece, Debbie (Natalie Wood), with even more determination and with a growing feeling of hatred for the Indians. Accompanied by the girls' adopted brother, the much younger and kindlier Martin Pawley (Jeffrey Hunter), Wayne spends the film hoping to find the girl, from the point when he knows that she will still be a little girl right up to when he realizes that she'll already be an adolescent and the wife of a Comanche. There's a scene in which Wayne goes to see some white girls who have been rescued by the army and who have probably lived with the

Comanches for as long as his lost niece. It's hard to tell if the girls are in a state of arrested development or have been driven mad, but one thing is clear, despite their fair hair and blue eyes, they have become completely Indianized. The look Wayne gives them before leaving the barrack hut where they're being held is perhaps the most chilling in the history of cinema, and it comes from an extraordinary actor with a remarkably wide range, an actor who, incredibly enough, a great many fools still caricature and damn with faint praise; in that one brief look there is hatred, grief, despair, sadness, pity and a desire for vengeance—all mixed up together. Wayne knows then that if he ever does find his niece, he will find someone not very different from these anomalous, alienated, half-mad girls with no place in the world, someone irrecoverable and incomplete. Each day that passes, therefore, counts against him, but he tracks and pursues her day after day, from the moment Debbie was taken and her parents murdered. And time, while it passes and we ride along on it, never ends. Not today or yesterday, but perhaps tomorrow.

When *Two Rode Together* opens, the time that Wayne experiences in *The Searchers*—the time on which he rides and against which he continues to fight with growing bitterness and with ever more sinister aims—is already over for the person doing the searching. Nine, twelve or even fifteen years have passed since the abduction of the white children and women whom a group of settlers now want to recover, encouraged by the vain and frivolous promises made by a congressman in Washington eager for publicity. The person charged with recovering the disappeared—or, rather, with haggling over them with the Indians and buying them back—has no blood ties with any of them. Unlike Wayne, Guthrie McCabe (James Stewart) is in no hurry and isn't filled with hatred or a desire for vengeance, nor does he have any personal interest in the matter. He is a mercenary who is prepared—most reluctantly—to carry out this mission and has no qualms about taking the life savings of the poor, confused settlers who initially welcome him as a Messiah who will restore to them their lost children and stolen womenfolk. But time has passed, and Stewart knows there's nothing to be done, that the process of uprooting and transformation will already be complete.

He knows that the five-year-old boy taken by the Comanches— frozen as a child in the memory of his family, who are in a similar position to Wayne, but lack his clear-sightedness—will now be a young warrior with stiff, stinking braids, that his chest will be covered with the scars inflicted on all Indian boys as part of their initiation into manhood, that he will have killed and scalped white folks and would rape his own fair-haired sister if he captured her. Stewart knows that the rosy-cheeked seven-year-old girl will be sixteen now and will have borne a couple of mixed-race children to some Indian brave, and that the mother lost by her good-for-nothing sons will have spent so long as the wife of an Indian that—as happens in Stewart's moving encounter with the woman who was once Mrs. Clegg—she will not even consider going back to her erstwhile husband and her now grown-up offspring ("Oh, no, no, don't tell them about me, they must never find me," she says to Stewart). In *The Searchers*, John Wayne, for all his hardness and anger and cruelty, still has some hope. In *Two Rode Together*, Stewart knows that there is no hope for the settlers. For him, they are people who are willingly deceiving themselves and who have equally willingly allowed themselves to be deceived by some congressman from Washington who has never even seen a real-life Indian. He therefore has no scruples about taking their money; he considers them mere dreamers, who will not learn until they see with their own eyes what their longed-for children and wives have become. Lieutenant Jim Gary (Richard Widmark), who accompanies him and urges him on, to some extent shares the settlers' good faith and hopes, but realizes when he sees the captives that Stewart has been quite right to oppose the whole impossible, propaganda-driven mission. He understands that they cannot force Mrs. Clegg to come back with them; she's an old woman whom they must not and cannot expose to what, for her, would be terrible shame. The same is true of young Frieda Knudsen, who has had two children by a Comanche; they are her present and her future; and the past with her white parents is literally and irrevocably just that, the past. *The Searchers* and *Two Rode Together* complete each other and in a sense take their place as a pair of films that rank among the high points of the Western and of the history of cinema as a whole. The difference is that, in one of these films, time is still passing, and, in the other, time has stopped. It's not hard to imagine which is the more bitter.

(2008)

Travelling Between Eternities

Critics who aspire to being always bang up to date have been prattling on for some years now about certain TV miniseries, saying, among other things, that they're far more adult and more complex than most big-screen films. I have to agree that few things I've seen in the cinema have captured my attention in quite the way *The Sopranos* did, or *Band of Brothers*, *The West Wing*, *Deadwood* and *Mad Men*. On the other hand, I just do not see the point of *The Wire*, whose early episodes struck me as frankly plodding. And as for the much-lauded *Lost*, far from finding it adult and complex, I thought it somewhat facile and arbitrary. The prestige of the miniseries, however, does not extend to full-length features made originally for television, and yet, in the last ten years, I have seen two genuine masterpieces, which could stand alongside any made-for-cinema films. The only difference, perhaps, was their length (some three hours or more) and the fact that they went straight to DVD. I thus read no reviews or interviews, there was virtually no publicity, and so the general public probably never even knew of their existence. It seems odd that such masterpieces should go unnoticed, even by the most modern and astute of critics.

One of those TV films dates from 2002 and was John Frankenheimer's swan-song. Frankenheimer directed two of the best political films ever made—*Seven Days in May* and *The Manchurian Candidate* (the original version starring Frank Sinatra and Laurence Harvey, that is, not the ridiculous remake featuring Denzel Washington), as well as *Birdman of Alcatraz*. His final made-for-TV film was entitled *Path to War*, a thrilling depiction of the presidency of Lyndon Johnson, the grey man who replaced Kennedy, and his growing involvement in the Vietnam War. Michael Gambon plays the President, and Alec Baldwin and Donald Sutherland are equally unforgettable in their roles. It should be seen by anyone interested in that subgenre of political cinema, "the White House movie," or indeed in cinema in general.

The TV film I really want to talk about, though, is one I discovered in 2006 and which I watched again a few days ago . . . on DVD. As far as I know, this magnificent film has never been shown on the big screen. To my and other people's chagrin, very few Westerns get made nowadays, and those that do are rarely much to write home about (I'm not even that keen on Clint Eastwood's award-laden *Unforgiven*). *Broken Trail*, however, directed by Walter Hill and starring Robert Duvall, seems to me one of the best Westerns ever made, almost on a par with the work of John Ford, Howard Hawks and Anthony Mann. In the film, Duvall and his nephew are driving some horses to Wyoming and, as in every road novel or film from *Don Quixote* on, they meet various people along the way. Their most important encounter is with five young Chinese girls, some no more than children, and all of them virgins, recently arrived in America and speaking no English. They are destined to be sold as prostitutes. Various incidents cause Duvall, his nephew and the violin-playing cowboy travelling with them to feel compelled to take charge of the girls and make them part of their journey, with all the inevitable delays and complications this implies. The relationships between the cowboys and the young Chinese girls, with whom they can barely communicate, are among the most touching I have seen in a very long time, never overplayed and never sliding into sentimentality. It's the same with the nonrelationship between the now elderly Duvall and the mature whore (Greta Scacchi), whom he also takes under his wing, along with a Chinese gentleman getting on in years. Almost without realizing it, they come to form a strange, taciturn family, in which Duvall—playing an admirable character called Print Ritter—ends up, quite unintentionally, unheroically and naturally, taking on the role of kindly paterfamilias. He's not always kindly, of course. He's also perfectly capable of soothing his nephew's conscience after the latter has hanged a man or of killing one of a group of men caught selling infected blankets to Indians as a more efficient way of exterminating them. Nothing about this masterly Western is over the top or gruesome, as is too often the case nowadays. It has its moments of violence, adventure, danger, muted lyricism and excitement, but there are also astonishingly quiet moments, among them a conversation by a river between Duvall and Greta Scacchi, which will inevitably remind film-lovers of another famous conversation by a river between James Stewart and Richard Widmark in Ford's *Two Rode Together*. *Broken Trail* is one of those rare films, and getting rarer, in which one likes all the characters. They are simple, sensible, sober people, with good moral values and a sense of humour, but they are never cloying. As Duvall says when asked to give a funeral address: "Birth 'til death, we travel between eternities." Or, as he explains elsewhere in the film: "We didn't go lookin' to save no Orientals or a broke-nosed whore. It just happened. Sometimes you just gotta roll with what's thrown at you."

(2010)

A Hero from 1957

When I was a child, the *tebeos*, or "comic books," published in Mexico by Novaro and sold in Spain were, as for many boys of my generation, both my companions and my teachers. They weren't called "graphic novels" then, a term invented by those who feel ashamed of writing or drawing them and, therefore, ashamed of having been a source of pleasure and fantasy for many children and grown-ups, as well as being partly responsible for the literary vocation of many writers, including myself. For although I started reading books quite young, when I was about eight, I made little distinction between the novels of Salgari and Verne, Stevenson and Dumas, Crompton and Blyton, and the comic books of *Capitán Trueno*, *Tintin*, *Hazañas bélicas* or my favourites, *Rip Kirby* and *Big Ben Bolt*. Or, indeed, the Spanish translations of the American comics also published by Novaro: *Roy Rogers*, *Gene Autry*, *Hopalong Cassidy* with his white hair, *Superman*, *Batman* and even *Aquaman* (a ridiculous superhero who, if I remember rightly, wore an orange-and-green uniform of scales and fins).

These comic books were, of course, written in Mexican Spanish, which meant that I learned words never used in Spain, such as *abigeo*—"rustler." I discovered that the baddies and villains were *pillos* (for example, an adventure might begin: "A gang of *superpillos* are planning to attack Metropolis"), and that they didn't just kill, they "bumped people off" or "took them out." Many of these adventures must have been adaptations from television series, as became clear when Novaro started publishing comic books, still with drawings inside of course, but with cover photos of actors disguised as detectives or gunmen. It was on one such cover that I first saw Clint Eastwood, who, pre–Sergio Leone, had costarred in a series entitled *Rawhide*. And then there was *Maverick*, my particular favourite, with James Garner; *Wagon Train*, some episodes of which were directed by John Ford; *Cheyenne* with Clint Walker; *The Rifleman* with Chuck Connors; *Gunsmoke* and *Tales of Wells Fargo*. And *Have Gun—Will Travel*, the series that triggered these memories.

Some of those TV series were also shown in Spain, but I never saw them, because my parents, who were strict about intellectual matters, as followers of the Institución Libre de Enseñanza tended to be, refused to have a television in the house until I was about seventeen, and, by then, I was already staying out late with my friends.* This meant that I didn't see any of the programmes my classmates talked about so endlessly, including *The Saint*, *The Fugitive*, *Bonanza* and *The Untouchables*. It's something that has always rather stuck in my gullet, so when my brother Fernando (the art historian) made a present to me of the first two seasons of *Have Gun—Will Travel* on DVD, I couldn't resist spending the summer watching them. The title refers to the words on the business cards that the protagonist, Paladin, hands out when offering his services

---

* The Institución Libre de Enseñanza was an educational and cultural institution founded in 1876 on the principles of secularism, coeducation, academic freedom, sporting activities and manual work or handicrafts. It had a lasting influence on culture and higher education in Spain at the end of the nineteenth and the first half of the twentieth century, even after it was shut down by Franco in 1939.

as a hired gun. The series began in 1957—fifty-five years ago, almost prehistory—and continued until 1963. The actor was Richard Boone, a man long past the first flush of youth, who always wore black when working, and had a slightly upturned moustache, a cleft chin and a craggy face. The music was written by Bernard Herrmann, much admired for the scores he wrote for Hitchcock (*Vertigo*, *North by Northwest*, *Psycho*); Sam Peckinpah wrote a script or two, and Charles Bronson, Angie Dickinson, Vincent Price and John Carradine put in guest appearances. Some episodes are more amusing or ingenious than others, but the best thing about them is the character of Paladin, and what we don't know or aren't told about him.

Paladin is a permanent resident in a luxurious hotel in San Francisco, where he scans the provincial newspapers to see who might need his services, for which he usually charges a thousand dollars. He doesn't wear black when in San Francisco, but dresses like a distinguished gentleman, plays poker and goes to the opera with various ladies whom he approaches in the foyer and then subsequently ignores. There are suggestions that he's from Boston and studied at West Point, that he left the army as an officer, possibly after the Civil War. He's a good strategist (his emblem is a chess knight) and has travelled quite widely: he knows London, Paris and even Madrid; he speaks Chinese and Spanish, can play a Verdi aria on the piano, has ridden camels and hunted tigers. Possibly rather too eventful a life for a man his age, but that's heroes for you. He's a bachelor, although he does come close to falling in love with a feisty lady doctor on the prairies. The most intriguing and striking thing about him, at least as far as I'm concerned, is that he's a very well-read gunman: in the midst of gunfights and shootouts, he quotes Shakespeare, Ben Jonson, Ecclesiastes, Homer, Sophocles and Pliny, Montaigne, Lamartine and Cervantes, he recites poems by

Donne and Browning, Byron and Keats, and in one episode he saves Oscar Wilde. He is a hard-bitten, but good-humoured man, whose normally implacable expression is often replaced by a generous smile. Sometimes, if he doesn't like the methods or intentions of the person hiring him, he changes sides. People often talk today about the golden age of television, but there were already small gems like these, modest and unpretentious, in 1957.

(2012)

Those Who Are Still Here

I recently had a truly Proustian experience, not the kind that simply makes you remember or recall something, but one that transports you, quite implausibly, to another time and, above all—and even more strangely—to another age, in my case to the remote age of four or five years old. It all started with some music: I came across the original soundtrack to one of the first films I ever saw, in fact, even though it wasn't the *very* first film I saw (I believe the first was George Sidney's *The Three Musketeers*, with Gene Kelly in the role of D'Artagnan and Lana Turner as Milady), I still think of it like that, possibly because I saw it several times when I was a small child and because it simultaneously provoked in me feelings of delight and feelings of sadness and melancholy. I put the CD on when I got home, and suddenly there I was, four or five years old again, and, despite having seen *Lili* many times, I was carried back to one particular occasion, to the María Cristina picture house in the Chamberí district—near Calle Covarrubias, the street where I lived and was born—accompanied by my mother and my brothers. The María Cristina picture house didn't survive, unlike others in the area, like the Colón in Calle Génova or maybe the Luchana, which perhaps even now exists, and to which I could, therefore, have returned when I was much older; however, the María Cristina—like the Príncipe Alfonso, also in Calle Génova—closed its doors when I was still a child, and so I didn't have that many opportunities to "shut myself away" in those particular auditoria, for that was what you did when you went to a cinema, you shut yourself away from reality. Anyway, hearing the soundtrack again made me think that the sadness it provoked both then and now is a characteristic I doubtless share with many of my fellow human beings—or perhaps not so many of them now—and is not in the least original. Different things will provoke that same sadness in different people, but I think I first became aware of it when I saw *Lili*.

I borrowed the video from my brother Miguel, and watched the whole film again all these years later. *Lili* was made in 1953, and its music—its theme song—was very famous in its day, so much so that almost anyone born in that decade would be sure to recognize it and be able to sing along. It was written by Bronislau Kaper, a great composer, European and classically trained, as were most of the composers who worked in Hollywood at the time. The director was Charles Walters, who made some fine musicals, and the actors were Leslie Caron and Mel Ferrer, with the outrageous Zsa Zsa Gabor in a supporting role. The film has lasted well and still has genuine charm, and even though it was made for children—with a major part being played by four puppets to which the ventriloquist Mel Ferrer gave voices—it's nevertheless tinged with a certain melancholy, as are all films about the circus or about fairgrounds, but my childhood feeling of sadness arose from a scene towards the end of the film when Lili decides to leave her job at the puppet show. She sets off alone with her suitcase along a vaguely dreamlike road, and suddenly—it's a figment of her imagination, but children can't really distinguish between the imagined and the real—the four puppets she had so reluctantly left behind appear at her side, except that now they're the same size as her. The music at this point is bright and cheerful, and the five of them set off together, so that the child viewer thinks: "Oh, good, they're all there and can keep each other company wherever they go." Then, when Lili dances with one of the puppets, it turns into Mel Ferrer and vanishes into the mist shrouding the road. After a few seconds of bewilderment and sorrow, the four remaining characters continue on, less blithely now, until Lili dances with another of the puppets, and the metamorphosis and disappearance is repeated. "They're getting fewer and fewer," thinks the child with growing anxiety, until the same thing happens to all of the puppets, one after the other. Reynard the Fox was my favourite, a suave fellow, who was also a liar and a thief.

"That," I thought a few days ago, "must be where my dislike of disappearances comes from." I never want anyone to disappear or go missing, not even those who have hurt me or who are poisoning our country. I've often been amazed at my own reaction on hearing of the death of someone for whom I felt not the slightest liking or admiration, even someone who has done his best to make my life impossible, for I've felt unexpectedly sad, as if my reaction were: "Yes, all right, maybe he was a real pest, but at least he belonged to *before*. He's been around for as long as I can remember, certainly long enough to become part of the landscape; I could depend on him; he was one of the cast, and it's just dreadful not to have him around any more." It's a feeling we're all familiar with to some extent: nothing is more dismaying than to discover that something—however unimportant—has changed or disappeared from a city we haven't visited for a while or from the district where we spent our childhood, and our sentiments then are along the lines of an outraged "How dare they!" because we experience any such changes as an attack on our own orderly world and on our own personal memory of the place: a stationery-shop-turned-bank, a cinema transformed into a hamburger joint, a lovely building replaced by an architectural eyesore . . . Not to mention people: you gradually come to realize that life consists in large part of watching those around you disappear, of feeling momentarily bewildered and sad, and then, like Lili and her fast-diminishing band of puppet companions, resuming your journey along the dreamlike road with the few blessed beings who remain, and who are still here.

(2007)

Why Don't They Come Back?

I don't see a lot of Spanish cinema, and I lay the blame for this, in large part, on the exaggerated patriotism of the Spanish press and of Spanish film critics. Years ago now they decided that *there simply must be* several Spanish masterpieces of cinema every season, but, unable to decide which films were masterpieces, they decided to praise to the skies any and every film made in Spain. To listen to them, anyone would think that there was a pool of talent in this country comparable only to 1950s Hollywood, when the "pool" included, to name but a few, Alfred Hitchcock, John Ford, Billy Wilder, Anthony Mann, Otto Preminger, Joseph Mankiewicz, John Huston, Stanley Donen, Vincente Minnelli, Samuel Fuller, Richard Brooks, Leo McCarey and, occasionally, Orson Welles. The reality, it seems to me, is quite different, and when I do get up the courage to go and see another of these supposed works of genius, I find something that is merely soppy or kitsch or stupid or pretentious or silly or crude, or else a copy of something much better that was made long ago and which, given the cinematographic illiteracy of the semi-young and the wilful forgetfulness of the older generation, no one recognizes as being a copy (there was a recent notable example of one such "masterpiece" which slavishly reproduced the atmosphere and characters from British director Jack Clayton's film *The Innocents*, adapted from Henry James's *The Turn of the Screw*—with Deborah

Kerr in the Nicole Kidman role—absurdly retitled, on its release in Spain, *¡Suspense!*). So you end up not trusting any of them and tarring them all with the same brush.

Having railed against these overhyped Spanish films on more than one occasion, it is perhaps only right, therefore, that I should welcome a great film when I see one, as is the case with Almodóvar's *Volver*. It isn't the only Spanish film I've liked in the last decade. There have been at least three others: *Nadie hablará de nosotras cuando hayamos muerto* [*No One Will Talk about Us When We're Dead*] by Agustín Díaz Yanes; *En construcción* [*Under Construction*] by José Luis Guerín; and one which I think I'm right in saying did not, unlike the other two, attract nearly as much attention from the critics and the prize-givers: *Al sur de Granada* [*South of Granada*] by Fernando Colomo.

I've spoken before about the ancient phenomenon of ghosts. Over the centuries many have believed in these beings who resist leaving the world and can find no rest beyond death. Nowadays, almost no one *seriously* believes in them. Some of us pretend to believe in them a little, mainly because we do not wish to discredit a literary genre that has produced some genuine masterpieces. Others mix them up with the various esoterica currently in vogue, but those who embrace *all* the exotic or anomalous beliefs that have ever existed (from horoscopes to Templar legends) tend to be bewildered, ignorant sceptics who don't really believe in anything and are simply trying them on for size. *Volver* is a ghost story and remains so to the end, because, despite the explanation given in the penultimate section, which puts everything back in its rational place, the return of Raimunda and Sole's mother continues to function like a spell or enchantment and continues to belong to the realm of fantasies, of the improbable and the marvellous. The reason why *Volver* is so moving as well as so funny, and the reason why it works so well from start to finish, is possibly because it speaks so naturally of domestic ghosts, which are the ones who appear most often in dreams, the only territory where they really do appear.

We all dream now and then of our dead. We see them so clearly, we hear their laughter, we talk to them, and sometimes, as Milton said in his sonnet about his dead wife, they're so vivid that day, when it wakes us, brings back our endless night. There exists a fantastical dimension to life which is in no way at odds with the rational one except when the two become fused, and in that dimension everything is imaginable, even what really happened. Indeed, in my opinion, what really happened only becomes truly real once we have imagined it, that is, once we have told it to ourselves as if it were a story. In that double dimension, that of the lived and the imagined, which Almodóvar's film explores, everything is perfectly straightforward and normal, almost sociological, a world of women accustomed to having to cope with even the worst situations with unexpected energy and pragmatism; there are lots of women like that everywhere. And yet, without it in any way undermining that normality, something extraordinary happens to them, something fantastic, or something, at least, which is experienced as such and is immediately incorporated, without contradictions or difficulties, indeed almost gladly, into the problems of everyday life. That's why it leaves an echo in those who see the film; that's why it resonates in the memory, why it invites us to fantasize, to imagine the potentially liveable and to live the potentially imaginable, and to ask what we all, slightly dreamily, ask ourselves from time to time, when we think of our dead: What would we do if they came back? Where would we put them? What would we want to ask them now? What would they think? What would they say to us? Why don't they come back?

(2006)

Music for the Eyes

Artistic prejudices are always the most difficult to root out. Critics—whose duty should be to see beyond the pretensions of artists and the public's passing fancies—often allow themselves to be persuaded by the way authors present their work, by what they say they have achieved, or else are guided by whatever has been a wild success—usually in order to take the opposing view—and which has been damningly labelled "popular." So, in literature, it has taken almost a hundred years since the death of Robert Louis Stevenson for critics and scholars to consider his work to be "serious" and to notice that one of his greatest admirers was Henry James, a writer who has always been venerated in academic circles. The fact that Stevenson wrote several brilliant novels enthusiastically devoured by children and adolescents—especially *Treasure Island*—was enough for him to be despised and for those same critics to forget that he was also the author of *Dr. Jekyll and Mr. Hyde* and other extraordinary tales, as well as essays that were far more penetrating and profound than any written by the very critics and professors who dictate what does or does not deserve to be studied and respected.

Something similar—Stevenson is just one example among many—is beginning to happen with a music that has traditionally been the object of scorn and dubbed not just "popular," but hybrid, subaltern and servile, namely, film music. As everyone knows to their cost, the symphonic music that people used to enjoy ended at the beginning of the twentieth century with Webern or possibly Schoenberg. With a few exceptions—Stravinsky and occasionally Bartók—the line indirectly linking Mozart and Wagner was broken, not as far as composers were concerned—for they felt they were being entirely consistent—but certainly as regards listeners. Serious contemporary music is quite simply impossible to listen to. It does exist, but only for a minority audience that would have seemed unimaginably tiny to Beethoven or Schubert or Brahms or Schumann, let alone Offenbach or Johann Strauss. It seems that, nowadays, there is only what used to be called "light music" in all its infinite varieties.

And yet the symphonic music that vanished with the twelve-tone system has lived on obscurely and modestly in cinemas, and people are now beginning to say as much out loud. You can buy records not just of the soundtracks of particular films, but also records by composers who mainly compose for the cinema, and who are, therefore, beginning to be taken seriously, just as happened with Stevenson not so many years ago. It is no longer considered eccentric or in bad taste to listen to recordings of music by Bernard Herrmann, an amazingly Wagnerian composer, who was responsible for the most chilling and the most lyrical moments in nearly all of Hitchcock's films, as well as in *The Ghost and Mrs. Muir*; or the great Miklós Rózsa, who composed one of the most romantic violin concertos ever, which can be heard in *The Private Life of Sherlock Holmes*, and the inspired scores for *El Cid* or *Spellbound*. It is no longer frowned upon to seek out records by Elmer Bernstein, whose soundtrack for *The Magnificent Seven*—which later became the theme for a cigarette ad—is familiar to everyone, but he was also responsible for the excellent symphonic soundtracks from *The Ten Commandments* and *Walk on the Wild*

Side; or Dimitri Tiomkin, who wrote the music for *The Alamo* and *High Noon* among others; or Korngold; or the amazing Victor Young, who wrote the soundtrack for *The Quiet Man* and *Johnny Guitar*; or the maestro Max Steiner, who was responsible for innumerable epic scores such as those for *Gone with the Wind*, *The Searchers* and *They Died with Their Boots On*. And even Henry Mancini, usually deemed too frivolous despite his undeniable talent—*The Pink Panther*, *Breakfast at Tiffany's*, *Hatari!* and *Charade*—is now admired by those in the know because of the complex score he wrote for Orson Welles's *Touch of Evil*. As you can see from their names, most of these musicians were of German, Russian or Hungarian origin, and had a very solid musical training.

However, this new interest is not confined only to Hollywood: in Italy, people express their unreserved admiration for Nino Rota, who composed for Fellini and Visconti; in France, the same goes for Michel Legrand and Georges Delerue—the latter wrote the soundtrack for *Jules et Jim*; in England, it's John Barry, who is best known for his Bond film soundtracks and for perhaps his best score: *The Chase*. Alex North—*The Dead* and *Viva Zapata!*; George Duning—*Two Rode Together* and *Picnic*; Jerry Goldsmith, Jerome Moross, André Previn, Lavagnino and Alfred Newman are all names that were once looked down upon, but whose work might become the classics of the twenty-first century. All that's needed is for the prejudice against their unpretentious music to fall away, music that people remember and even occasionally hum.

(1996)

Earthly Sighs

One unconditional crush usually excludes another, and my crush on Ann-Margret, when I was about fourteen, rather rudely buried the enduring, but much more childish crush I'd had on Hayley Mills—the daughter of the British actor John Mills—who managed to rescue from saccharine sentimentality such Disney productions as *The Parent Trap* and *Pollyanna*.

Ann-Margret's irruption into the lives of adolescents in the 1960s was quite something. It was, I think, my first platonic love affair, which was only platonic because of the very different dimensions in which we moved, her and me and my classmates. That is, it was a frustrated carnal love affair, but a love affair nonetheless. It's not hard to understand even today: if you watch the video of *Bye Bye Birdie*, a wonderful musical comedy directed by George Sidney, and to which *Grease* owes an enormous amount, you will see that the first thing to appear on the Panavision screen, with no warning whatsoever (even before the credits), is a very young Ann-Margret in a dress made of some semitransparent yellow fabric and set against an intense blue background, singing and cavorting to the song "Bye Bye Birdie." This was an overwhelming sight on the vast screens of the old cinemas, especially for fourteen- or fifteen-year-olds, whose desires tend to be impossible to disguise.

Ann-Margret was also close enough to the childish model of that desire to allow for a smooth, unhurried transition from boyhood to adulthood. She was a fresh, healthy, very clean young girl; there was nothing grubby about her, and she was innocent enough to be ideal and naughty enough to be real, in one's dreams of course. That film was followed soon afterwards by *Viva Las Vegas* alongside Elvis Presley, again directed by George Sidney, and in which, perhaps because of her legendary costar, Ann-Margret seemed far more inaccessible and infinitely less innocent and more lascivious. It's worth remembering that she had appeared before this in *Pocketful of Miracles*, Frank Capra's farewell to cinema, a film, alas, that was deemed unsuitable for children.

It's interesting and highly indicative that she has still not been entirely forgotten, as have so many other transient idols of our youth, who disappear forever, having brought a little joy to a couple of years' worth of schoolchildren, not even a whole generation. She sang wittily and danced brilliantly, she had a sense of humour and knew how to send herself up; and she soon summoned the courage to play slightly older women, for example, in Norman Jewison's *The Cincinnati Kid* (Sam Peckinpah was the film's original director and he certainly left his mark) and Mike Nichols's *Carnal Knowledge*, a rather weak, pretentious film that owes its best moments to her and her brief appearances in the nude. It should be said that Ann-Margret deliberately put on weight for the role—a forerunner of Robert De Niro's wilful and much-applauded metamorphoses.

Overall, she was underused as an actress, and was also unlucky enough to have been working in the 1970s, the worst decade in the history of cinema. If I remember rightly, she suffered a bad fall while filming in Las Vegas and had to submit her childlike face to plastic surgery and, for a while, was absent from the screens. When she returned, her moment, even that of mere superficial popularity, had passed. Nevertheless, she still appears from time to time and has grown older very gracefully, as can be seen in *Grumpy Old Men*, alongside Jack Lemmon and Walter Matthau. Or perhaps I still look fondly upon someone whom I loved and desired as a youngster (when I was young and so was she). I remember that in the unstoppable succession of long-distance crushes, she was replaced in my sighs by Audrey Hepburn during that period of greater spirituality through which all adolescents pass; replaced, that is, in my more celestial sighs, but not, of course, in my more earthly desires.

(1996)

The Man Who Appeared to Want Nothing

What fascinates me about George Sanders is that he always gave the impression that he could have been somewhere else and not in the many films he appeared in or, indeed, in the film industry itself. It wasn't so much that he seemed scornful of the art that brought him fame and money as well as an Oscar, it was more that he seemed to have been dropped into that world against his will, which is why he couldn't take it seriously, like a nobleman destined to lead a nobleman's life, but who finds himself obliged to do an ordinary bourgeois job, comfortable but somewhat undignified, beneath his status and rather too easy. And given the few facts I know about his life, there may have been an element of that. As if he were a second Nabokov, he was born in the city of St. Petersburg—but seven years later in 1906—the son of a factory-owner and a horticulturist, both of whom were, I believe, British, and again like Nabokov, he had to leave Russia with the coming of the Revolution. I also know that, initially, he worked in the textile industry and as a farmer growing tobacco, and that only in the 1930s, in the Depression, did he begin to take on small roles in the theatre and the cinema, until he was signed by Hollywood in 1936 for the film *Lloyds of London*. Perhaps he was just that, a businessman exiled to a puerile fantasy world of heroes and villains in which the real life he had led gradually moved ever further off, becoming blurred or lost. I never thought anyone could outdo James Mason in the role of Humbert Humbert in *Lolita*, until, that is, I imagined George Sanders in the part.

He had a strange air of superiority about him, which could have proved disastrous for an actor, but not for him, perhaps because he soon began to specialize in playing rather aloof, mocking characters, and perhaps because, along with that sense of superiority came an elegant acceptance of the inferior world surrounding him. George Sanders could create a sense of unease and disquiet because he himself was someone who never gave in to self-deception—neither he nor his characters, who were, of course, never ingenuous or smug, still less self-indulgent. George Sanders could always tell good from evil, he knew about moral rectitude and, what's more, recognized it when he saw it. And yet he consciously removed himself from it, he wounded and mocked it, fought and perverted it, and hurt it if he could, although rarely physically. He wasn't a classic out-and-out villain as other wonderful supporting actors went on to be, for example, Jack Palance, Lee Marvin and the inimitable John Carradine. He was someone who could have been something else, someone like us, but who appeared to have chosen evil, or perhaps evil chose him. It wasn't in his blood as it was with those other actors or less eminent ones like Jack Elam or Neville Brand, he wasn't destined to play that role by his appearance or his manners or his character, which was neither irascible nor neurotic nor despotic nor resentful, but ironic and patient and often sarcastic. He didn't usually hit anyone or resort to violence—at most a slap—his sole weapons were his words and his attitude, cynicism rather than hypocrisy, and often nothing more than a hat and a pair of gloves. When he played a cruel character, he knew he was being cruel, he had chosen to be; when he played a coward, he was aware that the opposite of a coward also existed, and was a calm and tolerant witness to his own cowardice; when he played an intriguer, he knew by heart all the dirty rules of the game and allowed himself no vacillations, no regrets. What was so moving and troubling about him was that he accepted his character's evil nature for what it was and never excused or disguised it. He didn't delight in it, but rather incorporated it into his persona, as something that he could have avoided, but hadn't, as if resigned to bearing the consequences and seeing to its conclusion an option that was perhaps hard to assimilate on one far-off day that Sanders doubtless remembered perfectly, but on which he wouldn't allow himself to brood overmuch, far less feel any self-pity or regret about the day his life took a wrong turning.

Sanders wrote an excellent detective novel that I read ages ago now, *Crime on My Hands*, as well as an autobiography entitled *Memoirs of a Professional Cad*, which I haven't read. The novel contains an amusing parody of the films featuring the detectives The Saint and The Falcon, roles that he played a number of times and got so heartily sick of that, in the end, he managed to offload the latter role on to his older brother, the actor Tom Conway, known mainly for his appearances sporting an evil-looking pencil moustache in *Cat People* and *I Walked with a Zombie* (both directed by Jacques Tourneur), and who had far less luck in his career despite having the same chilling voice as his brother, that rich, suave voice that seemed to go from outside in, as if every word spoken in those cool, disdainful, indifferent tones involved a tremendous effort on his part to silence inside him warmer, more affectionate words that had been buried and forgotten forever when he chose the dark path. You can hear Sanders speaking when, in *I Walked with a Zombie*, Conway says: "Everything good dies here, even the stars."

Some women I know find George Sanders enormously attractive, although he didn't look the part of the romantic lead at all. He was too tall somehow and his head too large, and with his thin, receding hair, he didn't look young even when he was, and there was something rather mild and soft about him which belied the brazen, cynical behaviour of the characters he played. Rex Harrison called him a "perfumed parlour snake" in *The Ghost and Mrs. Muir*, in which he plays an unscrupulous cad, as he did in *Rebecca* and *All About Eve*. In that last film, he treated Bette Davis appallingly, slapped Anne Baxter and talked down to Marilyn Monroe better than anyone, even Louis Calhern (another marvellous supporting actor) in *The Asphalt Jungle*. He was equally memorable playing a monocled Nazi in *Man Hunt*, directed by Fritz Lang, with whom he also worked on *While the City Sleeps* and *Moonfleet*. He had a thin but somehow full mouth, as if it changed size and shape depending on the intensity of the feelings he was inflicting on others, a rather large and far from straight nose, a somewhat flaccid face, which became slightly doglike as he aged, a broad forehead, and mobile but sober eyebrows. His eyes were terrifying, icily mocking and woundingly impassive. If he never deceived himself, it would have been still harder for others to deceive him. Sanders was someone who saw and knew not only his own weaknesses, but, even more unbearably, everyone else's, and instantly too. Confronted by him, any other character—any other actor or actress—seemed vulnerable and naked and as if struggling to gain his respect. If someone was greedy or envious or cowardly, embittered or full of hate, Sanders would spot it at once; he knew who he could persuade or bribe and who he couldn't, and, in the latter case, he wouldn't even try. Sanders was a very knowing villain, perhaps the man who knew most about what went on around him, on screen that is.

In *Viaggio in Italia* (*Journey to Italy*), he had one of his few lead roles, alongside Ingrid Bergman and directed by Rossellini. The truth is that, as a fictional husband, he oozed unreliability, and yet one presumes he must have had a certain weakness for his second wife, the frivolous Hungarian actress Zsa Zsa Gabor, one of Hollywood's most celebrated husband-hunters, since the fourth and final Mrs. Sanders was her older and less famous sister, Magda Gabor.

He had divorced them all by the time he committed suicide, after his final years when he dragged himself, more ironically and loftily than ever, through various substandard made-in-Europe co-productions, some of them directed by my uncle, Jesús Franco, who had some excellent tales to tell about that professional cad. He killed himself in Spain, in a hotel room in Castelldefels, if I remember rightly—in harsh exile—from an overdose of sleeping tablets. He left a note complaining that he was bored and in which he addressed the world in the same scornful, pitiless tone he had so often used in the cinema: "I am leaving you with your worries in this sweet cesspool." That was in 1972, when he was sixty-six. Perhaps that was the only time when he really wanted something, because the frightening feeling George Sanders communicated in his performances was that he seemed to be a man who knew what everyone else wanted, even before they knew it themselves, while he appeared never to want anything.

(1996)

The Supernatural Master of the World

Film "baddies" who began their careers in supporting roles and then, at some point in their careers, went on to become stars, often lost their most admirable qualities in that rise up the ranks. The most obvious and most painful example of this is Lee Marvin, who, after winning an Oscar for what was his worst performance, continued to be hard and grim-faced (although slightly less so), but was never again properly perverse. None of his subsequent performances contain half the cruelty, madness and sadism that made him such a favourite with more enlightened filmgoers in, say, *The Man Who Shot Liberty Valance*, *The Big Heat*, *Bad Day at Black Rock*, *The Killers* and even *The Comancheros*.

The great Vincent Price is a completely different case in several respects. True, he did go from being a supporting actor to playing lead roles, but he never won any awards that would allow him to take himself too seriously and he never starred in any big-budget productions. In fact, he gained enormously from his promotion to stardom without ever losing any of the striking characteristics cultivated and honed in his days as a lowly bit-part player. In films like *Laura*, *Leave Her to Heaven* or *While the City Sleeps*, before he began to specialize, he was a clumsy, overly tall figure, whose build only accentuated the contrast with the characters he played: devious, cowardly creeps lacking all integrity or nobility. Not that Vincent Price renounced those qualities in his later incarnations; indeed, he preserved his easy capacity for treachery, meanness and cowardice, while simultaneously acquiring and developing other previously unnoticed characteristics, which he elevated to almost canonical status. We have grown far too accustomed in recent years to seeing the "baddies" or the "monsters" as rather attractive characters with an element of pathos about them that arouses our pity or even sympathy. However, that "type" did not always exist. We felt pity for the poor monster in James Whale's *Frankenstein*, but not fascination. The precursor, the inventor of that "type" was Vincent Price.

Vincent Price endowed his characters with what one might call greatness, because there is no real greatness without irony, a quality Price had in spades, an irony aimed both at others and at himself. Forget the burlesque humour of *The Comedy of Terrors*; in his more or less serious roles, in *The Tomb of Ligeia* or *The Master of the World*, Price's mocking cynicism is evident in almost every scene, but always mingled with its possible contrary: a kind of hidden nobility. Vincent Price succeeded in doing what few actors in any genre have managed to do, namely, he gave us the immediate, unequivocal impression that he had a past, that he was once quite different from the person he appears to be—the vengeful criminal or the crazed megalomaniac. I can think of only one other actor who shared that ability—although he used it quite differently—and that was John Wayne, from *The Quiet Man* to *The Searchers*. It is a quality to be found only in the truly great actors. It is a rare gift that expands and multiplies an actor's resources, because it allows the viewers to see not only what the plot wants us to see, but also affords us a glimpse of what is being concealed or kept from us, so that we can enjoy both the actual performance and what lies hidden outside the time of the film.

Vincent Price often played very contradictory characters, men who are both taciturn and histrionic, wary and salacious, sullen and grandiloquent, fierce and amusing, solemn and comical, and those who consider him repetitive, limited or monotonous are quite simply wrong. He could play any register, it was just that his mastery of them was such that he ended up combining them all into one higher register, that of his own imposing physique, his own name. Like John Wayne, he was an actor who, however rich in variety and resources, never erased himself, as Alec Guinness and Laurence Olivier did and John Gielgud did not. Vincent Price was always Vincent Price playing someone else. But far from seeming monotonous, I would say that he could have played any role without ever ceasing to be himself. There is something almost Shakespearean about him, because, in common with many of Shakespeare's villains, even at his most vile and malevolent, he seems touched with genius. It is a shame he was never cast as Richard III or even Macbeth, roles he would have doubtless played as, respectively, evil and pusillanimous, but always with that touch of greatness.

With his large nose and piercing blue eyes, his full lips, always halfway between sorrow and sarcasm, his smooth moustache and arched eyebrows which he could wield like sabres, Vincent Price created a prototype and a lineage, whose most recent offspring is the young Dracula played by Gary Oldman and directed by Coppola: the man who is as sinned against as sinning, as wounded as he is wounding, as enthusiastic as he is disillusioned, as ruled by his past as he is firmly installed in the present that is leading him to damnation and ruin. The ending of *The Master of the World* provides a perfect illustration of the Price character, because he definitely came to be his own best character: the captain of the airship, the victim of his own obsessions, sits alone in his chair, contemplating the sky and waiting for the moment he will crash and be consumed by fire along with his grandiose dreams. He has sat there at other moments during the film, doubtless pondering his past. That is something Vincent Price will ponder now until the end of time, with his supernaturally generous smile and his steely, melancholy gaze.

(1994)

What If You Had Never Been Born?

One day last Christmas, I was doing about four things at once (don't worry, one of those things wasn't writing this article, I find even music incompatible with writing), and, as I sometimes do, I had the television on mute. I'm sure you've done the same thing, and it's a real test of those who appear on TV; if you take away voice and rhetoric, both of which distract enormously from the image, you can see with cruel clarity which politician is lying—even if we have no idea what he's talking about—which writer is spouting vacuous nonsense even he does not believe, which dancers can't dance for toffee, and which actors should long ago have retired. With a few notable exceptions—De Niro, Connery, Eli Wallach in one of his rare appearances, Keitel, Matthau, Caine—modern-day actors tend to be distinctly unimpressive, like film stars out of the Ark, who can't even look or walk memorably, who gesticulate as if they were still stuck in the age of silent films. When put to the same test, however, most older actors positively ooze authenticity and appear not to be acting at all, but to be there, alive, with us as witnesses to their troubles.

On that particular Christmas Day, and as usually happens around that time, one channel was showing Frank Capra's famous film *It's a Wonderful Life*. It was made more than fifty years ago, and whereas a book that was still being read after all that time would immediately be labelled a classic (especially in this impatient age of ours), it seems that, because film is a comparatively young art, critics find it harder to trust the sanction bestowed by time; and so, even though almost everyone loves that film, it isn't always acknowledged as a masterpiece. I wasn't intending to watch it for the eleventh or twelfth time, because I know it almost by heart, but its actors, even when deprived of voice and dialogue—James Stewart, Lionel Barrymore, Donna Reed, Gloria Grahame, Thomas Mitchell and the angel Henry Travers—immediately caught my attention and drew me in. It did not take long for me to restore the sound, abandon my other tasks (which included frying an omelette), and sit down and watch it to the end, such is its intensity, complexity and power to convince.

And I realized how superficial, obtuse and repetitive critics can be sometimes, because they have often criticized the film for being too ingenuous and optimistic, a crowd-pleaser. There is, in fact, only one ingenuous detail: the town that would have existed had James Stewart not been born—and that we see during his memorable stroll through what did not happen—is far more exciting—full of houses of ill repute and gambling dens—than the "real" town in the rest of the film. As for its supposed optimism, that is present only in the film's closing moments, but it is there solely because the protagonist has seen what he has seen and will never forget. The film is not just extraordinarily complex as regards narrative and time, it is also chillingly ambiguous; and it does not attempt to explain anything about the grave matters it touches on: identity, being and not being, the real and the hypothetical, memory as something not individual but shared, as a condition of its existence or validity, the possibility of never having been born, which has appealed so much to certain philosophers. And we have rarely been shown the pure horror experienced by James Stewart during his dreadful hours of nonexistence—if, that is, he *is* experiencing it, because if he hasn't been born, who is seeing this world in which he has never set foot? The horror of being denied by everyone and hearing over and over from the lips of the people he most loved: "No, you're not you, you're no one, I don't know you, I have no husband, I never had the son you want to be." The film is wrapped around by a vast zone of horror and darkness, which is even there in the happy ending. Perhaps surprisingly, it also contains one of the most erotic scenes I know, when Stewart and Reed are both listening on the same telephone, their heads together. And as for being "too popular," it was very nearly a gigantic flop when it opened in 1946: the audience found it too pessimistic for the Christmas period and left the cinemas feeling upset and troubled and pondering their own lives, uneasy and distressed by the abyss that the film's creator had opened up before them and made them peer into, or, worse still, in which they could see themselves reflected.

(1998)

The Ghost and Mrs. Muir

There is something peculiar about *The Ghost and Mrs. Muir*, a peculiarity shared, I think, by few other films, in that we desperately want the protagonist to die, even though we bear her no ill feeling at all. On the contrary, the character played by Gene Tierney—Lucy Muir—is an instantly touching figure from the very first moment she appears, when, having been a widow for a year, she decides to leave her unpleasant sister-in-law and her mother-in-law in order to go and live by the sea with her small daughter, Anna (Natalie Wood), and the old maidservant she brought with her when she married, Martha (Edna Best). With the income from some gold shares left to her by her husband, the late Edwin Muir, she intends renting a house in Whitecliff-by-the-Sea. At first, this seems like a feeble act of rebellion, a modest escape, as does her decision to shut herself away. Lucy Muir is going to withdraw into a tiny, female world, in which one would assume nothing unexpected would happen, as if—rather than quickly and easily embracing widowhood—she were regressing to a state of adolescent waiting and hoping: a vague and possibly hopeless wait, an empty wait, letting the doubtless monotonous days pass, with the only change being Anna growing up and Mrs. Muir and her maid Martha gradually growing older. Lucy Muir comments how useless she feels, adding: "Here I am nearly halfway through my life and what have I done?" to which

Martha retorts: "I know what *I* done, all right . . . cooked enough steaks to choke an hippopotamus." Lucy's comment about her uselessness is just that, a comment, not a complaint. In a way, you could see Lucy Muir as someone who is not so much resigned as reconciled to her lot: a conventional marriage, affectionate rather than passionate; a daughter for whose existence she takes no credit ("She just happened"); a death that didn't even take away her reason for living or cause her to fall into despair; silent acceptance, an absence of desires: perhaps that is what being reconciled to one's fate means.

Mankiewicz's film is, however, a film about words, about their power, their ability to enchant and persuade as well as to incite, seduce and enamour. It isn't only about that, of course, but it's certainly *also* about that. The ghost who inhabits the house, the ship's captain, Daniel Gregg—who has Rex Harrison's magnificent face— immediately infects Lucy Muir with his slightly coarse, sailor's vocabulary. One night, in the middle of a storm, Lucy goes down to the kitchen to boil some water, and the candles and the matches she tries to light keep going out; she angrily challenges the ghost to speak and show himself, calling him a coward. That is when Captain Gregg makes his first appearance as, first, an audible voice, then, a visible presence, and Lucy accepts him at once, asking only to be given a moment to get accustomed to the idea. And in that same conversation—in which the ghost is still slightly threatening in his manner as he explains why he haunts the house that was once his (a rather feeble plot device: he wants the house to become a home for retired sailors, which is why he doesn't want any tenants)—Lucy becomes annoyed and, to show her annoyance, repeats the captain's favourite word three times: "Blast! Blast! Blast!," the first symptom of contagion. Verbal contagion, that is.

This scene incorporates two of the film's other fundamental

elements: the natural acceptance of the dead as an active presence and the potency of inanimate objects and their capacity to *choose* the living and people in general, and not just, as is commonly believed, the other way round. Even though he is dead, has no material existence, no body—as he himself points out, "I haven't had one for four years"—Lucy immediately acknowledges the captain as the true owner of the house, which, in fact, officially belongs to a cousin of his, to whom Lucy pays the rent. When the captain proposes that they make a bargain and tells her that she can stay, that he won't drive her out, she responds with gratitude, as if she had received the blessing and the permission of the genuine owner, the spirit of the house, because things belong to the person, whether living or dead, whom they *choose* to belong to, and not the other way round; the worldly convention of legal possession has no real importance, but is merely a formalistic, bureaucratic hassle that one must dodge, avoid or fight. To Lucy it is immediately obvious that the house she is living in, and for which she pays rent, belongs to the captain, who designed and built it, and she therefore accepts his world without hesitation, as an act of justice. The captain, in turn, despite his initial response, agrees to let her stay because Lucy tells him that the moment she saw the house, she felt it welcoming her, as if it were waiting for her. The captain understands this, for he remembers having the same feeling when he stood before his first ship, which he found "rusting in the Mersey, gear all foul and a pigsty below" and recalls how she sailed twice as sweetly for him as she would for any other master, out of gratitude, words that could have been drawn from Conrad's memoirs (especially *The Mirror of the Sea*), in which he speaks at length about the sensitivity of ships, their gratitude, their refusal to be mistreated, their understanding of the character of their captain, their ability to recognize and feel betrayed or supported by the person in charge. That is why the house, called Gull Cottage, suddenly appears as a ship, not just in the characters' imaginations, but in the viewer's imagination too, helped by the proximity of the sea and by the telescope that presides over Lucy's room, in which most of the scenes that she and the captain appear in take place, and which is, in effect, their room. The captain promises not to leave that room and not to frighten Anna, on condition that Lucy moves his portrait in there ("It's a very poor painting," she says. "It's *my* painting," retorts the ghost).

From that point on, they lead an almost conjugal life. Even though she can see and hear the captain, Lucy immediately grasps that he is pure spirit and so she happily gets undressed and goes to bed in a room that is not only haunted, but inhabited by him. Even on the first night, when the ghost's voice makes some appreciative comment about her figure (which he has obviously studied at his leisure), she barely protests, because the captain is a spirit, albeit a talking one, a figment. One of the most extraordinary aspects of *The Ghost and Mrs. Muir* is that the two characters are fully conscious of the two different dimensions in which they move—the physical and the illusory—and they never rebel against them. It would have been a simple enough way of tugging at the viewer's heartstrings if either character had made a fruitless, despairing attempt to touch or embrace the other. This never happens; they never touch, and the impossibility of any contact is never underlined, the frustration and horror of wanting contact but never achieving it is never made visible, or only in that early scene, when they are both in the kitchen and Lucy goes over to him, pleased because she's being allowed to stay in the house, and he stops her, warning her to keep her distance, but this might simply be because they don't know each other and because, in England, at that time, people didn't usually shake hands, still less kiss or embrace by way of greeting, nor does that scene insist on their different material or immaterial natures. And yet that is the main cause of the heartbreak contained in the story being told: we know this and know it well enough for it not to be shown visually.

I described the story as heartbreaking, and in my view it is, despite the happy ending, because that ending lies outside the story itself, even though it is necessary and in no way seems like an addition or a sop to the audience. From the moment one accepts that the living and the dead can live together in the world, that happy ending is the only possible one, but it doesn't make what happens to the characters *during* the film any less sad, especially what happens to Lucy Muir. As the captain says at one point, he has unlimited time at his disposal (one assumes he doesn't even have such a thing as "time"), but she, of course, does not: time in her dimension—the only one she knows and that she can, therefore, imagine for herself—is limited and must be made the most of, because there will be no other time, and the ghost, who has experienced both dimensions, knows this well: the time of the flesh and the body, the time of the living—real time—does not come back. There are several scenes in which Lucy rebels against the captain's slightly superior manner. When he tries to persuade her not to fall into the clutches of the seductive Miles Fairley, the children's author known as "Uncle Neddy"—an extraordinary performance by George Sanders—Lucy asks him if it's a crime to be alive, and if he feels so superior because he isn't. And the captain responds by saying that sometimes living is a great inconvenience because "the living can be hurt." Then, shortly afterwards, he adds: "Real happiness is worth almost any risk," and behind this confession lies his own decision to disappear.

The romance between Lucy and the captain is that of married

life, of habit, of long knowledge of each other, of growing trust, and the gradual discovery that one cannot do without the other. It is the romance of conversation, and it is perhaps appropriate to recall that, shortly before he died and when asked in an interview what he thought of present-day films, Joseph L. Mankiewicz said that what he missed most of all was the loss of the word: for him, the cinema was not just about image, but an inseparable combination of image and word, the latter, according to him, having been driven out in the 1970s and '80s. The relationship between Lucy and the captain is forged, initially, out of their day-to-day contact (Lucy sews, and instead of sewing in silence and alone, she chats to the ghost—who, unlike any real husband, has nothing else to do), and, later, out of their joint endeavour writing the autobiography that the captain decides to dictate to her so that she can earn enough money to enable her to buy the house, when the shares left to her by Edwin Muir plummet in value, leaving her penniless. It's through the story of the captain's life, *Blood and Swash* (Lucy is the physical intermediary, the one putting the words down on paper, although not without blushing occasionally) that she gets to know him and to begin "to miss him" and to regret not having coincided with him in constantly passing time, not to have seen him when he first went to sea at sixteen or even before that as a boy living with a maiden aunt who missed him when he left. One of the most moving moments comes early on, when Lucy Muir identifies with that aunt, who, according to the captain, must have thanked heaven to see the back of him and not have to clean her carpets so often. Lucy says nothing, and when the captain asks her what she's thinking, she says: "I'm thinking how lonely she must have felt with her clean carpets." Lucy knows what is happening, and so does the ghost. The Spanish writer Juan Benet wrote in one of his novels: "I have never understood why love always arrives so late for its appointment with the appointed person." Here love arrives even later than usual, when nothing can happen, when there is no possible plan for the future and everything is already in the past. When they finish writing the book, and Lucy realizes that she was happy while they were doing it, because they were doing something together, she asks the captain: "What's to become of us, Daniel? Of you and me?" and the captain's response leaves no room for doubt: "Nothing can become of me. Everything's happened that can happen." "But not to me," says Lucy, suddenly aware that *her* time continues to flow. And it is then that the ghost reminds her that she should go out into the world more, meet people, "see men," as he puts it.

But while that aspect of the story is quite heartbreaking enough, it isn't only that: it isn't the story of a love that arrives too late, that begins too late and will come to nothing; it's a story of renunciation, the renunciation of something that is only words and imagination, the renunciation of the unsatisfactory and the absurd, the dreamed or fantasized, the renunciation, above all, of memory. Lucy meets Miles Fairley, who courts and seduces her. There is a moment in the film when Bernard Herrmann's marvellous music (which stands comparison with even the finest soundtracks he composed for Hitchcock) announces the threat and the imminent end of her relationship with the captain in a very subtle way, while what we see on screen doesn't appear to suggest this at all: an old sailor, Mr. Scroggins, has just carved little Anna Muir's name on a piece of wood, saying that her name will remain there forever. Lucy is swimming in the sea, her daughter calls to her to come and see the present that Mr. Scroggins has made for her. That is all. It seems to be no more than a linking scene, tranquil, neutral and rather joyful (although the progressive deterioration of the piece of wood and the still intact name will give us an idea, later on, of the passing of the years). And yet the music is terrifying, at once nostalgic and ominous, apparently referring to what is going to happen as if it had already happened: that act of renunciation, the disappearance of the captain, his farewell and his fall into oblivion. Miles Fairley sweeps Lucy off her feet, and she finds him exciting and fascinating. The captain doesn't like him and is clearly jealous, although he denies this, saying: "Jealousy is a disease of the flesh," knowing full well that this is not strictly true. Martha doesn't like "Uncle Neddy" either and does everything she can to dissuade Lucy, until Lucy counters with the cast-iron argument: "But he's real."

In a film that is, at once, so measured, intense, sober and so full of lyricism as *The Ghost and Mrs. Muir*, it is hard to select particular highlights, *morceaux de bravoure*, but if there is one scene that stands out from all the rest, it is the farewell scene. The captain has decided to step aside and not get in the way of Lucy's "temporal time," even though she is still expecting or hoping that he will stop her planned marriage to the very real Fairley, her marriage to reality. When she is alone—having just explained to Martha why she loves Fairley, however conceited, erratic and even childish he may be, defects she is more than aware of—she goes over to the portrait of the ghost and says: "Well, Daniel, haven't you anything to say?" The captain's voice does not thunder forth as it did on so many other occasions; there is only silence, because he is already leaving. And then comes the farewell scene: Lucy is sleeping, and, as he so often has before, the captain enters the room via the balcony and talks to her, reproaching her, at first, for not being as sensible as he had thought, but then he adds: "Don't trouble yourself, my dear. It's not your fault . . . You've made your choice, the only choice you could make. You've chosen life." Then, in her dream, he orders her to forget him, so that tomorrow, "in the morning and the years after," she'll remember him only as a dream, a state of mind, an atmosphere that filled her and even prompted her to write a book, which, he tells her, she wrote entirely alone. The captain gives her not only the royalties, which he had already given to her in their mutual desire to preserve the house, but also his own story, the story of his life, which, from then on, she will believe she invented. This is a crucial moment in the film, because the ghost becomes doubly a ghost, or, rather, he becomes a "real" ghost by becoming an object in a dream as well as a fictional character, Lucy's creation. It's as if the ghost had died a second time, had vanished and was thus even less real, even more ghostly when he discovers that, despite being no one, despite having neither flesh nor body, he can still inflict harm. There is a kind of despair at life and the living, as if, even though dead and firmly established in a state in which nothing can become of him, and everything that can happen has happened, the part of him that still makes contact with the living, the part that is still alive in him—his words, his laughter, his company—remains tirelessly harmful and a hindrance. Before disappearing, before his second death, the captain allows himself a moment of nostalgia that clearly foreshadows the death of Roy Batty (Rutger Hauer) in Ridley Scott's *Blade Runner*, when the replicant regrets the fact that everything he has seen and experienced will die with him ("I've seen things you people wouldn't believe . . ."). Here, Captain Gregg looks at the sleeping Lucy and pronounces a few lines that could have come straight out of Eliot's "Prufrock": "How you'd have loved the North Cape and the fjords and the midnight sun, to sail across the reef at Barbados, where the blue water turns to green, to the Falklands where a southerly gale rips the whole sea white!" and he concludes: "What we've missed, Lucia! What we've both missed!"

The rest of the film passes quickly, although years and years go by, indicated, as I mentioned earlier, by the piece of wood bearing the inscription "Anna Muir" and by the shots of waves breaking endlessly on the shore and accompanied by Maestro Herrmann's now wild music. After this, it is Lucy Muir's much shorter skirt that tells us how much time she has spent alone. It's not long before Lucy discovers that Miles Fairley is already married and has two children, in a wonderful scene when she goes to visit him at his London address and is received by his wife (Anna Lee), who tries to console her, saying: "It isn't the first time something like this has happened."

Lucy's life, her time—the time of her physical life, the time allotted to her, the time that is subject to change and in which things can still happen—has flowed past in solitude and emptiness, although not filled with any nostalgic thoughts of the captain, who has freed her from having to remember him when he gave her his instructions before leaving via the balcony—an extraordinarily considerate gift. However, her life, her time, "real" time, has passed without love or flesh or body or words or conversation, in the hopeless state of hope and waiting that Lucy appears to have chosen at the very start of the film and from which she emerged with the intrusion into her life of Captain Gregg. One must assume that he has spent his timeless time waiting for a future identical to the past, waiting to "experience" what he has already "experienced," namely, the company of Lucy Muir, and that cannot happen as long as she remains among the living. His impatience, therefore, will have been directed at the past, a past that was not a past because he was already dead when it began.

Little Anna is now a young woman, who comes to visit her mother with the sailor to whom she is about to be engaged. And suddenly, in the conversation between mother and daughter, they both discover that the other also saw and knew the captain, or dreamed of him during that first year in Gull Cottage, the house by the sea. Both were in love with him, the little girl as a little girl, and the mother as a grown woman. And Anna says to her mother: "Perhaps he did exist, the captain. Wouldn't it be wonderful if he had . . . Then you'd have something to look back on with happiness." And her view of memory is exactly the opposite of the captain's, who sees memory as being the greatest source of *un*happiness.

There is not much more to tell. We again see the waves breaking on the shore, and Lucy Muir appears briefly, this time with very white hair. She still lives with Martha, both having grown old together—as it seemed they would at the very beginning of their adventure—both talk to each other in the simultaneously fond and tetchy spirit of those who have been too long in each other's company. Lucy has a granddaughter also called Lucy, who, as she learns in a letter, is about to get married. That scene is only an epilogue, the scene showing her peaceful, painless death, the moment longed for and expected, although not perhaps by her (or perhaps it was), and, of course, by the captain and by the viewer. The glass of milk is spilled, and the ghost will tell his beloved as soon as she is dead: "And now you'll never be tired again." He holds out his hand to help her up from the armchair in which she has died and, arm in arm, they leave the house where they first met and where they lived together.

This apparently happy ending is the only possible one in a film in which the supernatural is instantly accepted as natural, in which we must pass continually from one dimension to the other, not simply as part of the pleasure of the film, but as a means to understanding it. And yet, as I said earlier, the story of Lucy Muir and Captain Daniel Gregg seems to me one of the most heartbreaking in the history of cinema; the heartbreak is there in the words spoken by the ghost created by Mankiewicz and by screenwriter Philip Dunne, when the captain bids farewell to Lucy: "What we've missed, Lucia! What we've both missed!" The captain is anticipating, because not only did they miss meeting each other when there was still time and physical reality, not only did they miss the North Cape and the fjords and the midnight sun, but also the years of conversation and laughter and company that could have awaited them during the time allotted to Lucy, who, in choosing the living, ultimately chose nothing, whose life was thus wasted, spoiled: that was her fate, to be someone to whom anything could have happened, but nothing did, or perhaps only that state of hopeless waiting. *The Ghost and Mrs. Muir* is not a mere fairy tale or ghost story; and although its director, Joseph Mankiewicz, considered it a youthful experiment, in my opinion, he made a film—on a par with John Huston's *The Dead*—that goes much further in touching on something rarely touched on in the cinema or in literature: the abolition of time, the vision of the future as past and the past as future, reconciliation with the dead and with the serene, deep-seated desire to, at last, be one of them.

(1995)

Acknowledgements

The following is a list of the original title of each piece, the first place and date of publication, followed by its first inclusion in book form. All appeared, in the first instance in Spanish (for the most part), in the periodical press, before being collected subsequently in book form, also in Spanish, frequently in more than one volume. The first date of publication in the periodical press is listed, followed by the first collection in book form.

The main collections by Javier Marías cited here are (in cases of two editions, the pieces appear in both, unless a specific date indicates a given one):

Pasiones pasadas, Madrid: Anagrama, 1991
Pasiones pasadas. Edición ampliada, Madrid: Alfaguara, 1999
Vida del fantasma, Madrid: EL PAÍS/Aguilar, 1995
Vida del fantasma. Cinco años más tenue, Madrid: Alfaguara, 2001
Literatura y fantasma, Madrid: Siruela, 1993
Literatura y fantasma. Edición ampliada, Madrid: Alfaguara, 2001
Mano de sombra, Madrid: Alfaguara, 1996
Seré amado cuando falte, Madrid: Alfaguara, 1999
A veces un caballero, Madrid: Alfaguara, 2001
El oficio de oír llover, Madrid: Alfaguara, 2005
Demasiada nieve alrededor, Madrid: Alfaguara, 2007
Lo que no vengo a decir, Madrid: Alfaguara, 2009
Ni se les ocurra disparar, Madrid: Alfaguara, 2011
Tiempos ridículos, Madrid: Alfaguara, 2013

Acknowledgements

A Borrowed Dream

"A Borrowed Dream" ("Un sueño prestado," *El Semanal*, 5 February 2006; subsequently, in *Demasiada nieve alrededor*)

"Air-Ships" ("Aviones marineros," *Granta en español*, no. 1, 2004)

"The Lederhosen" ("Los pantalones tiroleses," *El País Semanal*, 27 November 2005; subsequently, in *Demasiada nieve alrededor*)

"An Unknowable Mystery" ("Un misterio incognoscible," *El Semanal*, 4 February 1996; subsequently, in *Mano de sombra*)

"Ghosts and Antiquities" ("Fantasma y antigüedades," *El País Semanal*, 9 November 2003; subsequently, in *El oficio de oír llover*)

"The Invading Library" ("La biblioteca invasora," *AD*, September 1990; subsequently, in *Pasiones pasadas*)

"Uncle Jesús" ("El tío Jesús," *Publicaciones Dezine*, no. 3, May 1991; subsequently, in *Pasiones pasadas*, 1999)

"Old Friends" ("Los antiguos amigos," *El País Semanal*, 5 November 2006; subsequently, in *Demasiada nieve alrededor*)

"I'm Going to Have Fun" ("Yo me divertiré," *El Semanal*, 27 June 1999; subsequently, in *A veces un caballero*)

The Most Conceited of Cities

"Chamberí" ("En Chamberí," *Diario 16, Cultura*, 14 July 1990; subsequently, in *Pasiones pasadas*)

"The Most Conceited of Cities" ("La ciudad más presumida," *Suplemento Semanal*, 4 November 1990; subsequently, in *Pasiones pasadas*)

"The Keys of Wisdom" ("El manojo de llaves de la sabiduría," *Liber* supplement in *El País, Le Monde, L'Indice, Frankfurter Allgemeine Zeitung*, 15 December 1990)

"Venice, An Interior" ("Venecia, un interior," *El País*, 22, 23, 24, 25 and 26 August 1988; subsequently, in *Pasiones pasadas*, and Penguin/Hamish Hamilton)

All Too Few

"Noises in the Night" ("El ruido en la imaginación produce monstruos," *El País Semanal*, 16 April 2006; subsequently, in *Demasiada nieve alrededor*)

Acknowledgements

"The Modest Case of the Dead Stork" ("El modesto caso de la cigüeña cadáver," *El País Semanal*, 13 September 2009; subsequently, in *Ni se les ocurra disparar*)

"Lady with Bombs" ("Cuento de la poderosa con bombas," *El País Semanal*, 13 June 2010; subsequently, in *Ni se les ocurra disparar*)

"A Horrific Nightmare" ("Una espantosa pesadilla," *El País Semanal*, 6 May 2007; subsequently, in *Lo que no vengo a decir*)

"No Narrative Shame" (in *Los intérpretes de vidas*, Santillana Ediciones, 2007)

"All in Our Imagination" ("Figuraciones sólo nuestras," *El País Semanal*, 12 October 2008; subsequently, in *Lo que no vengo a decir*)

"The Weekly Return to Childhood" ("La recuperación semanal de la infancia," *Diario 16, Gente*, 12 June 1992; subsequently, in *Vida del fantasma*)

"Why Almost No One Can Be Trusted" ("Por qué casi nadie es de fiar," *El País Semanal*, 7 June 2009; subsequently, in *Ni se les ocurra disparar*)

"In Praise of the Egotist" ("Elogio del egoísta," *Vogue*, May 1990; subsequently, in *Pasiones pasadas*)

"All Too Few" ("Siempre muy pocos," *El País Semanal*, 3 December 2006; subsequently, in *Demasiada nieve alrededor*)

Dusty Spectacle

"Damned Artists!" ("Peste de artistas," *El País Semanal*, 5 October 2008; subsequently, in *Lo que no vengo a decir*)

"Dusty Spectacle" ("Polvoriento espectáculo," *El País, Libros*, 18 November 1990; subsequently, in *Pasiones pasadas*)

"My Favourite Book" ("Mi libro favorito," *Diario 16, Libros*, 21 September 1989; subsequently, in *Literatura y fantasma*)

"This Childish Task" ("Esta pueril tarea," *El País Semanal*, 31 December 2005; subsequently, in *Demasiada nieve alrededor*)

"For Me Alone to Read" ("Para que yo lo leyera," *El País Semanal*, 10 June 2007; subsequently, in *Lo que no vengo a decir*)

"Hating *The Leopard*" ("Odiar *El Gatopardo*," *El País, Babelia*, 12 March 2011)

"Writing a Little More" (in Peter Holbrook, ed., *Shakespeare's Creative Legacies*, London: Bloomsbury Arden Shakespeare, 2016)

"Roving with a Compass" ("Errar con brújula," *El Urogallo*, September–October 1992; subsequently, in *Literatura y fantasma*)

Acknowledgements

"Who Is Who?" ("Quién escribe," abridged version in Marina Mayoral, ed., *El personaje novelesco*, Madrid: Cátedra/Ministerio de Cultura, 1990; subsequently, in *Literatura y fantasma*)

"Time Machines" ("Máquinas del tiempo," *El País Semanal*, 9 April 1995; subsequently, in *Mano de sombra*)

"The Isolated Writer" ("El escritor aislado," *El País*, Babelia, 3 September 2011); JM's acceptance speech on receiving the 2011 Austrian State Prize for European Literature in Salzburg

"Too Much Snow" ("Demasiada nieve alrededor," *El País Semanal*, 26 March 2006; subsequently, in *Demasiada nieve alrededor*)

"The Much-Persecuted Spirit of Joseph Conrad" ("El perseguido espíritu de Conrad," *El País Semanal*, 24 December 2006; subsequently, in *Demasiada nieve alrededor*)

"The Improbable Ghost of Juan Benet" ("Y el espíritu inverosímil de Benet," *El País Semanal*, 31 December 2006; subsequently, in *Demasiada nieve alrededor*)

Those Who Are Still Here

"The Hero's Dreadful Fate" ("El espantoso futuro del héroe," *El País*, Babelia, 16 July 2011)

"Riding Time" ("El tiempo cabalgado," *El País*, Babelia, 26 July 2008)

"Travelling between Eternities" ("Viajamos entre las eternidades," *El País Semanal*, 7 November 2010; subsequently, in *Ni se les ocurra disparar*)

"A Hero from 1957" ("Un héroe de 1957," *El País Semanal*, 9 September 2012; subsequently, in *Tiempos ridículos*)

"Those Who Are Still Here" ("Los que aún están," *El País Semanal*, 4 February 2007; subsequently, in *Demasiada nieve alrededor*)

"Why Don't They Come Back?" ("Por qué no vuelven," *El País Semanal*, 14 May 2006; subsequently, in *Demasiada nieve alrededor*)

"Music for the Eyes" ("Música en la retina," *El País Semanal*, 5 May 1996; subsequently, in *Mano de sombra*)

"Earthly Sighs" ("Suspiros terrenales," *Nickel Odeon*, no. 2, Spring 1996; subsequently, in *Vida del fantasma*, 2001)

"The Man Who Appeared to Want Nothing" ("El hombre que parecía no querer nada," *Nosferatu*, no. 20, January 1996; subsequently, in *Vida del fantasma*, 2001)

Acknowledgements

"The Supernatural Master of the World" ("El amo sobrenatural del mundo,"
Fantasiazko eta beldurrezko zinemaren astea, October–November 1994; subsequently, in *Vida del fantasma*)

"What If You Had Never Been Born?" ("De no haber nacido," *El País Semanal*,
8 February 1998; subsequently, in *Seré amado cuando falte*)

"The Ghost and Mrs. Muir" ("El fantasma y la señora Muir," *Écrire le cinéma*,
Éditions Cahiers du Cinéma, 1995; subsequently, in *Vida del fantasma*)

Margaret Jull Costa has been a literary translator for more than thirty years and has translated works by novelists such as Eça de Queiroz, José Saramago and Bernardo Atxaga, as well as poets such as Sophia de Mello Breyner Andresen and Ana Luísa Amaral. She has won various prizes, most recently the 2017 Best Translated Book Award. She is a Fellow of the Royal Society of Literature and holds an OBE for services to literature and an honorary doctorate from the University of Leeds.

Alexis Grohmann is Professor of Contemporary Spanish Literature at the University of Edinburgh. He is the author of *Coming into One's Own: The Novelistic Development of Javier Marías*, among other studies and edited collections of essays on Spanish and European literature. He is a corresponding member of the Real Academia Española.